Stanley R. Sloan
De-Trumping U.S. Foreign Policy

**De Gruyter
Disruptions**

―
Volume 1

Stanley R. Sloan

De-Trumping U.S. Foreign Policy

Can Biden Bring America Back?

DE GRUYTER

ISBN 978-3-11-075902-0
e-ISBN (PDF) 978-3-11-075943-3
e-ISBN (EPUB) 978-3-11-075946-4
ISSN 2748-9086
e-ISSN 2748-9094

Library of Congress Control Number: 2021946974

Bibliographic information published by the Deutsche Nationalbibliothek
The Deutsche Nationalbibliothek lists this publication in the Deutsche Nationalbibliografie;
detailed bibliographic data are available on the Internet at http://dnb.dnb.de.

© 2022 Walter de Gruyter GmbH, Berlin/Boston
Cover image: Fabio Ballasina / unsplash.com
Printing and binding: CPI books GmbH, Leck

www.degruyter.com

Dedication

This book is dedicated to the memory of Monika Hannelore Sloan, my beautiful wife and love of my life since 1973 when we first met in Vienna, Austria. Monika passed away during drafting of the manuscript for this book. She was not only my muse and companion for all those years but also the first one to review and suggest editorial changes for most of my drafts. The love we shared was our own "transatlantic bargain." Monika was a sincere, independent, loving, sensitive soul whom I will love forever, as I always promised. Rest in peace, my sweet princess.

Acknowledgments

In December 2020, I was honored when Anthony Mason invited me to submit a book proposal for De Gruyter Publisher's new "Disruptions" series. I had no idea then what the coming months would hold. My wife Monika was diagnosed with terminal cancer in February 2021, and I spent the next five months as her caregiver. Monika had been my first reviewer and editor for decades. She insisted I continue with work on this book.

I could not have completed this book without the stellar support of two Middlebury College students who volunteered to serve as research assistants for the project. Ideal Dowling, my former student since taking my Winter Term course on Euro-Atlantic Relations in January 2019, previously served as my research assistant for *Defense of the West: Transatlantic Security from Truman to Trump* (2020: Manchester University Press). Ideal was essential to the timely completion of the manuscript and immensely helpful in the publishing process. Joely Virzi was a student in my virtual Euro-Atlantic Relations course in January 2021. She demonstrated, as had Ideal two years previously, remarkable analytical and writing skills and enthusiastically accepted my invitation to join the team for producing this book. Throughout the process, Ideal and Joely have been meticulous researchers, skilled writers, perceptive editors and, most of all, dear friends. Both accomplished athletes – Ideal in squash and Joely in soccer and track – they displayed all the traits that make one a great team player. Their professional contributions and unwavering personal support enabled me to complete this work. They forever will have my sincere appreciation and heartfelt thanks. I know their talents will enrich the future for their families, friends, classmates, colleagues, and professions.

I also want to express my thanks to Anthony Mason, De Gruyter Publishers and my editor, Michaela Göbels, for affording me this challenging opportunity to contribute to their new series of books and for volunteering to allow me to dedicate the volume to Monika.

While I appreciate all the sources of assistance with this project, responsibility for any mistakes or roads not taken is, of course, mine.

Contents

Introduction —— XI

Chapter 1: Trump and America's role in the World —— 1
    The starting point —— 1
    Trump's narcissism —— 2
    Political philosophy and populism —— 3
    Authoritarian tendencies —— 5
    Inexperienced, unpredictable, incompetent, and corrupt —— 7
    The U.S. role in the world at the end of Trump's presidency —— 9

Chapter 2: Biden confronts the challenge of de-Trumping U.S. foreign policy —— 14
    Restoring American leadership: Biden's prime objective —— 15
    Diplomacy Rooted in Democracy: liberal democracy at home and abroad —— 16
    China: the leading nation-state challenger —— 17
    Russia: defense, deterrence, and careful cooperation —— 19
    North Korea: danger in a small package —— 20
    Iran, Middle East: a new focus —— 20
    Afghanistan: intending to head for the exits —— 21
    Cuba and Latin America: rejecting Trump unilateralism —— 22
    Immigration: seeking more humane approach —— 23
    Counterterrorism: working with allies —— 24
    Pandemic policy: top domestic priority influencing foreign policy —— 24
    Climate change: returning to the Paris Climate Accord —— 25
    Domestic "soft power" issues: fighting U.S. drift toward authoritarianism —— 26
    Foreign policy based on strong, united nation: Biden seeks bipartisanship —— 27

Chapter 3: Biden's beginning a mixed bag —— 29
    Restoring American leadership: the right words —— 29
    Diplomacy Rooted in Democracy: restoring relations with allies —— 31
    China: seeking multilateral support for hard line toward Beijing —— 32
    Russia: don't trust, do verify —— 33
    North Korea: seeking contact, unsuccessfully —— 34
    Iran, Middle East: back to the nuclear deal —— 35

Afghanistan: preparing to leave —— 36
Cuba and Latin America: frustrated with Cuban repression —— 37
Immigration: new policies, but dealing with a surge —— 38
Counterterrorism: new challenges after Afghan withdrawal? —— 39
Pandemic policy: administration's biggest early success —— 39
Climate change: building foundation for international cooperation —— 40
Domestic "soft power" issues: "building back better" —— 41
Foreign policy based on strong, united nation: it takes two to tango —— 44

Chapter 4: What obstacles stand in Biden's way? —— 46
Diplomacy Rooted in Democracy: restoring trust in U.S. model will not be easy —— 46
China: presenting a competing model to liberal democracy —— 50
Russia: still actively interfering in Western democracies —— 53
North Korea: small country presenting big problem —— 57
Iran, Middle East: Biden needs Iran, Saudis, and Israel to cooperate —— 60
Afghanistan: Taliban takeover challenges Biden leadership goals —— 62
Cuba and Latin America: not so easy… —— 64
Immigration: policy may not produce substantial results for a long time —— 66
Counterterrorism: terrorist threats with roots abroad and at home —— 69
Pandemic policy: anti-vaxxers/maskers risk Covid-19 resurgence —— 70
Climate change: no time to waste —— 72
Domestic "soft power" issues: economic revival depends on pandemic control —— 74
Foreign policy based on strong, united nation: many threats to unity —— 75
Restoring American leadership: still in question —— 76

Chapter 5: Why does it matter whether Biden brings America back? —— 78
In historical context —— 78
The bottom line —— 81
Democracy at home, key to leadership abroad —— 83

Bibliography —— 85

About the Author —— 92

Introduction

And so the world watches America – the only great power in history made up of people from every corner of the planet, comprising every race and faith and cultural practice – to see if our experiment in democracy can work. To see if we can do what no other nation has ever done. To see if we can actually live up to the meaning of our creed.

Barack Hussein Obama, *A Promised Land*

While Donald Trump was in office, trying obsessively to undo virtually everything that Barack Obama had done, Obama was writing the autobiography through his first term as president. The challenge raised by Obama early in his volume, reproduced above, was one that he did not expect to be met during Trump's presidency.

From Obama's perspective, his successor had put American democracy and creed in full reverse, erasing standards that had been set by Republican and Democratic presidents alike over many decades. Yes, the world was watching and wondering if the Trump presidency would be the future for the country that had once sought to lead the world, guided by the beacon of democracy and human rights. Rather than follow principles and values that had been accepted for years, Trump laid down a process of governance set on a purely transactional foundation. This appealed to enough Americans to get elected and then to govern for four years, but not enough to win a second term. The foreign policy implications of this approach to governance produced rewards for those countries that bowed down to Trump's personal and policy preferences and threatened distancing for those that did not. But, at least for the democracies around the world that had seen the United States as a model, the United States had abandoned this role, producing a huge vacuum internationally that could not be filled by any other nation.

The Trump approach to U.S. foreign policy, which oozed affection for several dictators and showered criticism on traditional U.S. friends and allies, very quickly dissipated what is known as America's "soft power," which provided the fuel required for countries to admire and follow the United States based simply on the essence of the nation. Professor Joe Nye is the established wizard of soft power. Some analysts and commentators apparently see soft power as anything that does not involve military forces. But that is off the mark. The term actually focuses on how aspects of that form of power affect the behavior of other members of a system, states in the case of the international system.

Chapter 1 of this book discusses the impact of his presidency on the U.S. role in the world. The discussion identifies continuities and discontinuities between Trump and traditional contemporary U.S. foreign policies. The chapter examines the influences that Trump brought to the oval office based on his personality, experience, and self-interests. It concludes that he left his successor, President Joe Biden, with a huge challenge of trying to rebuild the U.S. leadership role in the international system, regaining the trust of its main allies, and reorienting American foreign policy toward authoritarian regimes and leaders, whom Trump seemed to admire. This chapter includes evaluations of both elite and public opinion from America's democratic allies around the world and elite opinion only in states less friendly to the United States. It will distinguish between countries that appreciated Trump's approach (particularly Israel and Saudi Arabia), those that were particularly troubled by Trump's rejection of multilateralism and alliances (including Germany and many members of the European Union), and those that tried to use Trump's proclivities to advance their interests (including France, North Korea, Russia, and China).

The second chapter documents and evaluates Biden's approach to foreign policy and his goals for the U.S. role in the world. While this is a moving target, Biden's goals are quite well outlined in speeches and articles published during the presidential campaign and since, as well as during a long career as U.S. Senator and Vice President to President Barack Obama. The focus is on the Biden Administration's attempt to restore American respectability and leadership internationally. It accounts for the fact that not all the issues confronting Biden were created by Trump. Parts of the challenge either pre-dated Trump or were not caused principally by Trump's conduct of U.S. foreign policy.

This chapter also examines how Biden's domestic policy objectives, in the areas of the pandemic, systemic racism, political equity, the economy, immigration and climate change, relate to his foreign policy goals. To the extent that American soft power (using Joe Nye's definition) is dependent on these aspects of Biden's presidency, they will play into his attempt to restore America as a democracy worthy of emulation. The fact that the opposition Republicans decided to cling to the leadership of their defeated president creates special challenges, as does the fact that Biden's Democratic Party control of both the House and the Senate hangs on an electoral thread, threatening to snap in the 2022 mid-term elections. This chapter seeks to set the bar against which potential success and/or failure can be measured.

Chapter 3 documents the early steps toward implementation of the Biden foreign policy agenda. Given the schedule for publication, this chapter includes primarily actions taken between January and July 2021. It identifies important areas of continuity and discontinuity between Biden and Trump foreign policies.

Chapter 4 assesses the chances for Biden to succeed in achieving his stated objectives. It looks at the international and domestic obstacles to success and evaluates the chances of success or failure in each of the key areas of policy.

In some ways, the domestic challenges are even more daunting than the foreign ones. While foreign governments – friends and adversaries alike – help create the circumstances with which the Biden administration must cope, the domestic environment directly affects Biden's ability to govern and therefore to implement foreign and defense policies required by the objectives he has set. This Biden scorecard sets the stage for discussing the consequences in the next chapter.

The final chapter evaluates the potential consequences of success or failure in achieving the range of objectives that Biden has already established. It concludes that Biden's approach, if successful at home and abroad, can restore American respectability and leadership. But it cautions that success is not guaranteed and in fact may be no more than a 50–50 proposition.

Chapter 1
Trump and America's role in the World

This chapter analyzes how America's place in the world's eyes had changed by the time Donald Trump left office. Before approaching that challenge, however, the chapter first examines the component parts of Trump's international involvement that contributed to the nation's global status at the end of his presidency. Some elements of the 45th president's means and methods were present under previous presidents, but many aspects of Trump's approach to the world beyond American borders were uniquely shaped by his personality and priorities. The discontinuities introduced by Trump's unique foreign policy ideas and actions profoundly affected foreign governmental, elite, and public perspectives on the United States often in ways that disrupted America's ability to defend and advance its national interests.

The starting point

The Trump presidency began with anything but an empty international slate. Under his predecessor, Barack Obama, the United States built up a large reserve of soft power based as much on who Obama was as on what he did or promised to do. In most of the countries allied to the United States, the fact that the country had elected a relatively liberal racial minority politician who seemed to represent a wide range of common values and interests was perceived as a strength and positive for relations with his government. But Obama had also carried forward some baggage left over from his predecessor, Republican George W. Bush, the largest piece of which was the continuing conflict in Afghanistan. Bush had started the process of winding the war down, and Obama sought to continue that process, but he also got bogged down in the dilemmas posed by the choice between ending the war unconditionally or trying to do so on terms that could be described as a success, if not a victory.

Trump made it clear after his election that he would not be bound by anything that carried Obama's imprimatur. This determination held true in foreign as well as domestic policy. Most of all, Trump seemed to resent the level of popularity that Obama had enjoyed overseas, particularly with U.S. allies. He boasted an approach that he believed would not require such popularity, convinced of his own arguably mythical status as master of "the art of the deal." Trump believed that Obama had given away important American interests and that he could restore American strength and respectability with his talents finely honed by his business investment career, burnished by his role as a reality show host. The rejection of everything that Obama represented was one of the most important influences in the early stages of the Trump presidency. In cases where Trump was more-or-less following in the footsteps of an Obama policy, Trump's explanation was that he could do it bigger and better.

Trump's narcissism

Without going into scientific evaluations of Trump that concluded he was a malignant narcissist, it seems that Trump brought not just a rejection of everything Obama to the office but also an embrace of anything that could be labeled as Trump. To win the U.S. presidency, a candidate must have reasonably strong self-confidence. Trump was not the first American president to bring an inflated ego into the office, but his appeared to exceed any of his predecessors by some substantial distance.

The perception of Trump's narcissism challenged foreign leaders to assess how they could best advance their interests, and those of their countries, in dealing with the new American leader. Among U.S. allies, French President Emmanuel Macron developed the most distinctive approach. Macron decided that playing to Trump's ego would be the best means to promote France's interests. He invited Trump to enjoy France's Bastille Day (independence day) parade on July 14, 2017, featuring military units and much pomp and circumstance. But by the end of Trump's term in office, Macron appeared to give up on his attempt to form a special bond with Trump and was even caught on video during the NATO summit in London in December 2019 making fun of the American president with other allied leaders.

In addition, Germany's Chancellor Angel Merkel frequently clashed with Trump, at times simply appearing disgusted with his behavior and heavy-handed approach to relations with her country. Trump's critical attitude toward both Merkel and Germany was likely deepened by the fact that commentators early in his term began referencing Merkel as the new leader of the West. Perhaps the most graphic demonstration of Trump's narcissistic behavior came at the inaugural NATO summit at the alliance's new Brussels headquarters in May 2017 where he was caught pushing his way past other leaders, shoving Montenegro's prime minister out of the way in the process. The bottom line regarding this aspect of Trump's approach to international leadership is that he sought reinforcement of his high opinion of himself and was resentful of those who did not give it. For those whose predisposition was critical of the United States for abuse of its international power position, Trump's approach added more evidence to their perception of the United States not only as a hegemonic power but as an international bully.

As for Japan, the leading U.S. ally in Asia, a shock came quickly due to Trump's withdrawal from the Trans-Pacific Partnership (TPP), which was a key political and economic link for Japan to the United States and other Pacific trading partners. Japan's commitment to multilateralism and international cooperation is just as strong as that of America's European allies. Prime Minister Shinzo Abe responded to the jolt by factoring Trump's ego into his approach. According to one expert, "Breaking protocol, Prime Minister Abe organized a visit at Trump Tower ahead of the presidential inauguration. With the gift of a gold-plated golf club, Abe's strategy to charm Trump was born."[1] And so, Prime Minister Abe went down the same path as France's Macron. He did so presumably from fear of the damage that Trump could do to Japan's interests if he did not move quickly to ingratiate himself with the new American president. However, the approach seemed to have little impact on Trump's complaints about trade specifically or his burdensharing concerns that included Japan and South Korea as well as NATO Europe.

Political philosophy and populism

Candidate Trump ran very much as a "conservative" populist for the Republican Party. As was frequently noted during the campaign and after, Trump was not a life-long Republican but had at various times aligned with the Democrats or had presented himself as an independent. He was known to have donated to both Republican and Democratic candidates for office at many different levels.

The conclusion of most observers has been that Donald Trump has no real political philosophy. His alignment with populism seems to have been intended to win enough voter support to convince more traditional Republicans to see his victory in the primary contests as inevitable. If any philosophy could be found behind his actions, it could be said to be transactional informed by conservative rhetoric. The actions of Trump and his supporters in Congress did not necessarily follow consistent traditional Republican lines: the GOP prides itself on favoring a small role for government and controlling government spending. While Trump's rhetoric generally followed this line, the tax "reform" bill promoted by his ad-

---

1 Mireya Solís, "U.S.-Japan relations in the era of Trump: Navigating the turbulence of "America First," México y la Cuenca del Pacífico. Vol. 8, núm. 24 / septiembre-diciembre de 2019. Opinión invitada 9. https://www.brookings.edu/wp-content/uploads/2019/09/20190903_japan_us_relations.pdf [accessed June 23, 2021].

ministration and enacted with the support of a Republican-led Congress dramatically increased government deficit, largely to the benefit of corporations and wealthy individual businessmen and women.

Internationally, Trump did boast a policy guided by "America First." This slogan perhaps was the closest his administration came to what could be called a foreign policy philosophy. To the rest of the world, however, it presented challenges. "America First" had deep roots in Trump's populist domestic political strategy. His hard-core supporters seemed to love the pugnacious character of the approach, often on display at Trump campaign rallies in 2016 and throughout his presidency. Trump rejected the traditional U.S. role as the leader of the West because he did not want to make the compromises often required to develop multilateral approaches to international trade, economic, security and environmental issues. His rejection of the U.S. leadership role led some observers to judge that the "America First" concept had produced "America alone" outcomes. It also meant that Trump relied almost completely on "hard power," the ability to get others to act in support of certain interests through coercion and payment rather than through "soft power" – the ability to gain support for interests and objectives through "co-option," based on potential supporters' admiration and respect as well as perceptions of shared interests.

One of the most dramatic rejections of international cooperation was Trump's withdrawal from the Joint Comprehensive Plan of Action (JCPOA), an agreement designed to delay Iran's development of nuclear weapons that the Obama administration had negotiated with China, France, Germany, Russia, the United Kingdom, the European Union, and Iran. Trump intended to demonstrate a hard line toward Iran in leaving the deal, but there was no sign his approach had moved Iran away from acquisition of nuclear weapons capabilities. In fact, Iran moved more actively toward developing that capability. Trump's move clearly represented the rejection both of a major Obama administration accomplishment and of cooperation with our key allies, further evidencing America's unpredictability under Trump.

To allies of the United States, "America First" translated into burdensharing demands, threats and trade restrictions. Trump argued that friends and allies of the United States had been taking advantage of its generosity for years and promised that he was going to end that exploitation. The message received by traditional allies of the United States was that Trump-led America could no longer be counted on as a reliable ally. This understanding among allies inspired French President Macron – who, as noted above, sought to win Trump over by appealing to his ego – to try to rally other members of the European Union to strengthen Europe's "strategic autonomy" under French leadership. On the other hand, some traditional American adversaries were likely pleased at the disruption "America First" caused within the West while also being somewhat reassured about their interests by Trump's friendly outreach to them. Trump's administration aligned firmly with the undemocratic leadership of Saudi Arabia, Iran's leading enemy in the region along with Israel, whose then-prime minister Netanyahu strongly supported Trump and his message.

Trump's radical right populism aligned him internationally with growing strength for like-minded politicians around the world.[2] The phenomenon was particularly strong in Europe, where radical right politicians came to power in several countries, including Poland, Hungary, and Turkey. If Trump had an international leadership role, it was largely one of setting an example that facilitated the rise of other radical right populists. It remains to be seen if the rejection by a clear majority of Americans of Trump will take some of the steam out of the radical right movements in other countries.

Authoritarian tendencies

Combining Trump's populist approach with his narcissistic personality leads to another factor in his approach to governance: the tendency toward authoritarianism. One of the major themes of Trump's attitude toward the world during his presidency was a focus on his alleged ability to make "deals." In his business and media activities he claimed to have succeeded because of his mastery of the "art of the deal." During his campaign for the presidency, Trump often declared "I alone can fix it." As one observer pointed out, "*I am your voice*, said Trump. *I alone can fix it. I will restore law and order.* He did not appeal to prayer, or to God. He did not ask Americans to measure him against their values, or to hold him responsible for living up to them. He did not ask for their help. He asked them to place their faith in him."[3] The sure-fire path to authoritarian rule is convincing the public to put their faith in one leader, rather than their own values, precedent, the rule of law, or the political system.

Trump seemed to believe that he could apply his experience not just to domestic policy, but also to his relationships with some of the world's leading authoritarian heads of state, including Russian President Vladimir Putin, Chinese President Xi Jinping, and North Korean Supreme Leader Kim Jong-un. In his

---

[2] For a detailed discussion of Trump's populism in the context of the broader spread of radical right politics see the author's *Transatlantic Traumas: Has illiberalism brought the West to the brink of collapse?* (Manchester University Press, 2018).

[3] Yoni Applebaum, "I Alone Can Fix It," *The Atlantic*, July 21, 2016. https://www.theatlantic.com/politics/archive/2016/07/trump-rnc-speech-alone-fix-it/492557/ [accessed June 23, 2021].

meetings with such counterparts, he seemed to value their degree of control in their countries and therefore their bond with him. He most notably went so far as to tell the world in a now-infamous press conference after his meeting with Putin in Helsinki that, regarding possible Russian interference in the 2016 American elections, he trusted Putin's word more than the conclusions by the U.S. intelligence community.

Because the U.S. political system divides power among three branches of government – the executive, legislative, and judiciary – some American and foreign observers hoped that the network of constitutional and political "guardrails" represented by the separation of power would protect the country against a president intent on building his own power. To some extent the system did put up obstacles to most of Trump's authoritarian instincts, but with the Congress controlled by the Republican Party, which was largely becoming a Trump fan club, and the Supreme Court rapidly being populated by conservative judges nominated by Trump and fast-tracked to confirmation by then-Senate Majority Leader Mitch McConnell, many observers began to worry that those supposed guardrails were no longer as reliable as they had once thought. Trump's mistrust of the government structure he came to head resulted in attacks on career government officials. This led to retirement and resignations of many key officials, particularly among seasoned career diplomats at the Department of State, seriously weakening the institution and U.S. diplomatic capacity in general.

It turns out that the constitutional system of protections against a president gathering excess power is very dependent on political decisions of other elected and appointed officials, most of whom owed their jobs and future potential to the president. Moreover, President Trump had one major national media outlet – Fox News – that he could count on to promote and defend his decisions, to the point where Trump opponents began referring to Fox as "state TV." Even the role of the rest of a free press as protection for safeguarding democracy seemed to be diminished by the mainstream media's fascination with and coverage of this unique American president, despite his constant attacks on media sources that did not fall in line.

The system's guardrails, despite being put to their most severe test in American history, stood up through the Trump presidency. Whether they would have survived a second Trump term is an open question. The Trump campaign claim that the election had been stolen – known as "the big lie" – sought to delegitimize Joe Biden's victory. Trump's promotion of the insurrection aimed at preventing congressional certification of the election outcome further demonstrated the former president's authoritarian tendencies and motivations. In 2021, it is possible to suggest that the tendency of the United States toward a more authoritarian form of government has been slowed, if not stopped. But the rest of the world, particularly U.S. allies, has remained uneasy about the future, wondering if the country has truly returned to a path on which democracy can be promoted and strengthened.

Inexperienced, unpredictable, incompetent, and corrupt

Virtually any American presidential administration is likely from time to suffer from one or more of these criticisms. But the Trump administration, in the eyes of the world as well as to many at home, seemed prone to a wide range of such defects.

On the question of experience, Trump probably came up shorter than any other president in American history. He had never served in public office, did not serve in the military at any level, and had never run a political organization. Many of his supporters touted his "business" experience and know-how as bringing a valuable type of expertise to the presidency. But others pointed out that Trump had basically been given a golden handshake by his successful and rich businessman father and that Trump always ran a family-type corporation, never having to deal, for example, with boards of directors or shareholders. He was accustomed to being in total control, as exemplified by his famous catchphrase from his television show: "you're fired." This kind of business experience could be another factor feeding his authoritarian temptations: there was never anyone to whom he had to account for his business decisions, except when he was sued by former customers, employees, contractors, and the like. In those cases, he usually managed to eliminate problems with a good team of lawyers and plenty of money behind the defense.

Because Trump brought no real political philosophy into the presidency, as noted above, it was difficult to predict what courses he might take domestically or in foreign policy. He was known to follow most generally a "transactional" strategy: doing what is beneficial for one's own interests, uninformed by political philosophy or values. Trump and his administration were also unpredictable in the sense that he had no respect for precedent, the political system and its bureaucracy, or the constitution – except when it served a transactional political purpose, such as in opposing any form of gun safety measures. Other nations, whether friendly or adversarial, rely to some extent on being able to anticipate the directions likely to be taken by such a major power as the United States. Adversarial powers like Russia and China undoubtedly appreciated the extent to which Trump's unpredictability weakened U.S. leadership of the West and relations with U.S. allies, undermining American power and influence abroad.

The perception of incompetence in the Trump administration, starting at the top, further undercut U.S. foreign and security policy leadership internationally. It was an open secret that Trump had great difficulties in attracting mainstream Republican talent to serve in his administration, and so the results of the nomination process were spotty. If political appointees in the administration did not attract widespread international respect, the U.S. government and its foreign and defense policy agencies did manage in many respects to carry forward more traditional policy lines, even as Trumpian winds blew overhead.

This was the case particularly regarding the North Atlantic Treaty Organization (NATO). Candidate Trump had not only attacked U.S. NATO allies for their insufficient contributions to the alliance but even suggested that the United States should honor its commitments under the North Atlantic Treaty only if the country in need was seen as "paying its dues." This suggestion raised the very fundamental questions of whether the United States would honor NATO's Article 5 mutual defense commitment if another ally were attacked, as the United States was on 9/11, when the allies did invoke Article 5 and came to the defense of the United States. It also raised the specter of NATO becoming completely ineffective or destroyed if the United States were to change its commitment or, in the most extreme case, leave the alliance under Trump's management. Despite these ominous currents from the top, the Department of Defense and State Department civil servants largely kept the alliance in business, even increasing U.S. commitments in some areas. Trump's anti-NATO and anti-German instincts broke through at the end of his administration when he ordered a large reduction in the U.S. presence in Germany, but the process had hardly gotten underway when a more NATO-friendly government came to office under President Biden.

Finally, power inevitably has corrupting effects on mere mortals and sometimes even on previously acclaimed and accomplished ones. In the Trump case, a degree of corruption was built into the administration's culture by Trump's business background and connections, many of which were brought into his government via political appointments. Perhaps most notably in Trump's presidency, corruption via family connections seemed to have outdone any previous examples. This came into play most directly in the case of his son-in-law Jared Kushner, who was given influential roles in a variety of foreign and defense policy areas, but most notably in managing the U.S. relationship with Saudi Arabia. Kushner became close friends with Saudi Prince Mohammed bin Salman, increasing U.S. arms sales to Saudi Arabia and intensifying shared opposition to Iran. The close ties and hands-off approach adopted by the Trump administration seemed to protect the Saudis against any criticism or punitive actions from the administration, even when it was shown that a Saudi assassination team had killed Washington Post correspondent and Saudi citizen Jamal Khashoggi to silence his criticism of the Saudi regime.

As for his daughter Ivanka, she was assigned to represent the United States at international meetings and was given special treatment for her business interests by foreign governments, including that of China which reportedly fast-tracked large numbers of her trademark requests after Trump came to office and she became an "unpaid" White House advisor to the president.[4] The full extent to which Trump, Ivanka and Kushner personally benefitted financially from corrupt practices during their time in office may never be known, but they certainly left behind a long trail of questionable practices of using one's government positions to benefit their own financial interests.

The U.S. role in the world at the end of Trump's presidency

If American power is measured only by defense spending and military capabilities, the Trump administration's performance might receive some passing grades. The president and his administration did put a major effort into increasing U.S. defense spending and promoting new weapons systems. It did arguably promote U.S. national security objectives with selective use of force and opposition to some antagonistic regimes, like the one in Tehran, Iran. The hard power of the United States remained understood and considered as an important factor in foreign policy and security calculations by friends and foes alike.

But on the question of soft power, it was a different story. International respect for the United States went from relative highs at the end of Obama's second term to dramatic lows in the early stages of the Trump administration. According to a Pew Research Center survey of citizens from 37 countries, at the end of the Obama presidency a median of 64% stated that they had confidence in the U.S. president to make the right choices regarding foreign policy. Early in the Trump presidency, only 22% expressed such confidence. The survey also asked about America's image. At the end of Obama's presidency, a median of 64% held a favorable view of the United States. Early in the Trump term, the median had dropped to 49%. Notably, there were only two countries in the survey that gave Trump higher marks than Obama: Israel and Russia. (See Figures 1, 2)

---

4 Tommy Beer, "Ivanka's Trademark Requests Were Fast-Tracked In China After Trump Was Elected," Forbes, September 22, 2020. https://www.forbes.com/sites/tommybeer/2020/09/22/ivankas-trademark-requests-were-fast-tracked-in-china-after-trump-was-elected/?sh=77da0a0c1d60 [accessed July 25, 2021].

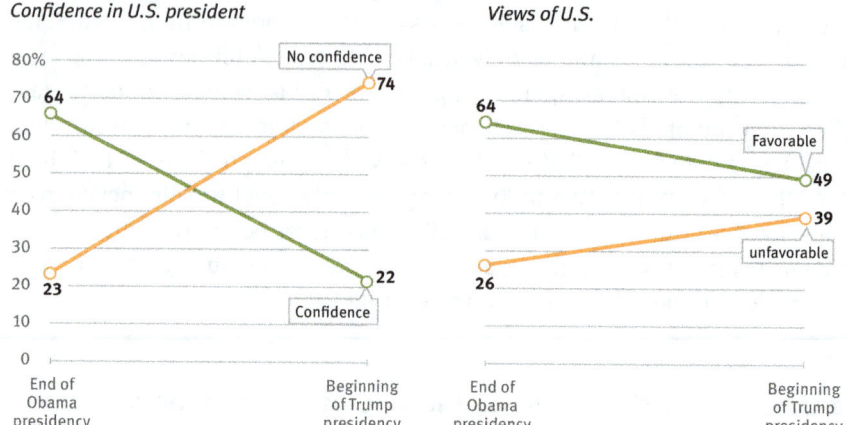

Figure 1: Low global confidence in Trump leads to lower ratings for the United States. Source: "U.S. Image Suffers as Publics Around World Question Trump's Leadership," Pew Research Center, Washington, D.C., June 26, 2017. https://www.pewresearch.org/global/2017/06/26/u-s-image-suffers-as-publics-around-world-question-trumps-leadership/ [accessed August 18, 2021].

As the Trump administration neared its end, the Pew Research Center released the results of a survey of citizens of 13 major countries, all democracies that are allied to or friends of the United States. The survey found that only 24% of those surveyed had a favorable view of the United States. The survey also measured the confidence levels of these countries in President Trump. The median confidence level was a staggering 16%. Germany was particularly low at a 10% confidence level: only 1 in 10 Germans had confidence that Trump would do the right thing in foreign policy.[5] The large reservoir of American soft power that existed at the end of the Obama administration had been almost totally depleted.

---

[5] Richard Wike, Janell Fetterolf, and Mara Mordecai, "U.S. Image Plummets Internationally as Most Say Country Has Handled Coronavirus Badly," Pew Research Center, September 15, 2020, https://www.pewresearch.org/global/2020/09/15/us-image-plummets-internationally-as-most-say-country-has-handled-coronavirus-badly/ [accessed June 27, 2021].

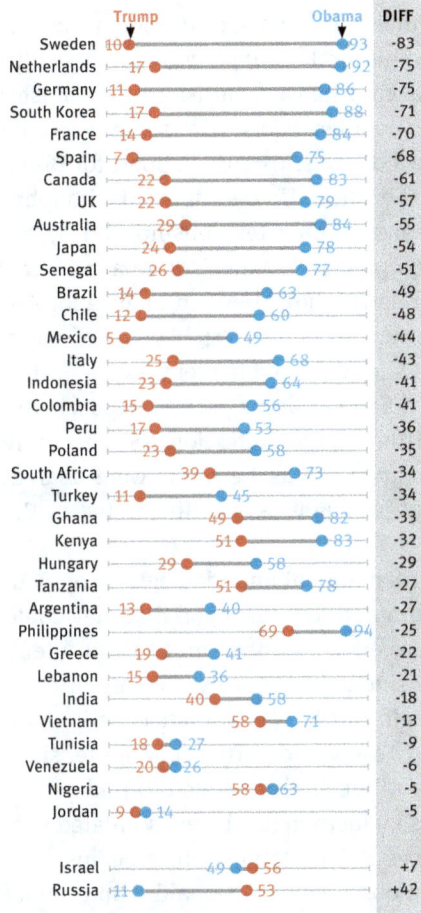

Figure 2: Trump global ratings lower than Obama's. Source: "U.S. Image Suffers as Publics Around World Question Trump's Leadership," Pew Research Center, Washington, D.C., June 26, 2017. https://www.pewresearch.org/global/2017/06/26/u-s-image-suffers-as-publics-around-world-question-trumps-leadership/ [accessed August 18, 2021].

Even in democracies, public opinion does not always determine governmental perceptions or policies. It can be said, however, that while allied governments continued to work constructively with the Trump administration, they were not happy with the way he treated them or their nations. The fact that key alliance heads of state were caught on video making fun of Trump behind his back at the London NATO summit in December 2019 was a tip of the iceberg: allied leaders were clearly rooting for a Trump loss in the 2020 elections and for Joe Biden to take over the reins of power in Washington.

As noted earlier, some allied leaders did their best to convince President Trump to avoid producing a disaster in their relationships. President Macron made the most overt show of his effort, but his strategy apparently produced little in the way of gains for France or for Macron himself. British Prime Minister Boris Johnson emerged politically from populist roots like those used by Trump, and they started out on relatively good terms. Trump's support for Brexit – the United Kingdom's departure from the European Union – sat well with Johnson and formed one of the early foundations for their relationship. But by the end of Trump's presidency, Johnson seemed prepared to move on to a more traditional American partner in the "special relationship." German Chancellor Angela Merkel could easily be imagined producing a huge sigh of relief when Trump lost the 2020 election, ensuring that she could end her term as chancellor with a more agreeable partner in the United States. For his part, NATO Secretary General Anders Fogh Rasmussen played Trump quite professionally, frequently praising the American president for accomplishments he knew were shared, not Trump's alone, but understanding that he might be standing between the American president and NATO's demise.

As for relations with America's main international and ideological competitors, China and Russia, both Presidents Putin and Xi understood that they could use Trump's narcissism to their advantage. Perhaps Putin, with his KGB intelligence training and experience, was best positioned to maneuver Trump into positions that favored Russia and Putin himself. But Xi was also effective in managing China's relationship with the United States under Trump. More tensions and conflict were involved than with Russia, but Xi also seemed to understand that he could best defend Chinese interests by factoring in Trump's inflated ego.

Looking back at the Trump presidency as Biden's term in office begins, British strategic thinker Sir Lawrence Freedman observed that "Donald Trump's final disgraceful weeks in office displayed him at his narcissistic worst, encouraging the storming of the Capitol by his supporters, and leaving a legacy of damaging claims about the electoral process that will take time to dispel…" Freedman judges that Trump actually accomplished very little in foreign policy, except perhaps to raise difficult questions about the stability and predictability of the United States as the leader of the West. The American people rejected Trump in 2020, but Freedman muses that America's allies were left wondering: "what would happen with a future president with similar prejudices and policies but also more intelligence, competence, and discipline?"⁶

In the meantime, the country was moving on, preparing for a new and vastly different presidency under Joe Biden, a career Democratic politician with extensive foreign policy experience and a determination to return the United States to more traditional lines of U.S. foreign policy.

---

6 Lawrence Freedman, "Trump's Limited Legacy," H-Diplo/ISSF Policy Series 2021–42, June 25, 2021. https://issforum.org/roundtables/policy/ps2021–42 [accessed June 25, 2021].

Chapter 2
Biden confronts the challenge of de-Trumping U.S. foreign policy

Joe Biden came to the presidency not only with substantial victories in the electoral college as well as the popular vote but also with a career filled with experience in both domestic and foreign policy issues. His public service journey consists of 36 years as a member of the U.S. Senate, including serving as ranking member and then chairman of the Senate Committee on Foreign Relations, and two terms as Vice President for President Barack Obama. Along the way, he negotiated with foreign leaders – friends and foes alike – was deeply involved in NATO issues, and spent endless hours strategizing and formulating his approaches to the U.S. role in the world.[7]

Having served in two branches of government that play leading roles in the formulation and execution of U.S. foreign policy, Biden was certain to have a reasonably well-developed set of foreign and defense policy concepts, principles, and, perhaps most importantly, instincts. This immediately set Biden apart from his White House predecessor, whose only true foreign policy experience came during his term as president.

Of course, there are downsides as well as advantages to having extensive experience in any line of work. Joe Biden has acknowledged that his choices on major foreign policy issues were not always the right ones, at least with the advantage of hindsight. The author's former CIA colleague and subsequent Secretary of Defense for both Presidents George W. Bush and Barack Obama, Bob Gates, wrote less generously in 2014: "I think he has been wrong on nearly every major foreign policy and national security issue over the past four decades."[8] One might have thought that Gates's extensive intelligence background would have induced more discretion with such expansive evaluations, but it is

---

[7] The author was fortunate to have worked with/for Senator Biden both to produce a variety of Congressional Research Service studies on national security issues requested by Biden and as support for the Senate NATO Observer Group, which Biden co-chaired, during the process of NATO's first post-Cold War enlargement. I was given floor privileges for the Senate's consideration of that enlargement, a debate that Biden managed.
[8] Philip Bump, "Robert Gates Thinks Joe Biden Hasn't Stopped Being Wrong for 40 Years," The Atlantic, January 7, 2014. https://www.theatlantic.com/politics/archive/2014/01/robert-gates-thinks-joe-biden-hasnt-stopped-being-wrong-40-years/356785/ [accessed June 27, 2021].

clear from Gates' book[9] that he and Biden, and Biden's top staffers, clashed frequently when they were serving in the Obama administration.

Without doubt, the list of Biden decisions that can be regarded as "wrong" is worth noting. As a senator in 1991, he voted against the Persian Gulf War, which most see as a successful operation, and then in favor of the 2003 invasion of Iraq, which most think was a major mistake. As Vice President, he has acknowledged he advised against conducting the raid that killed Osama bin Laden – not because he opposed the objective but because the operation seemed based on uncertain evidence of bin Laden's presence at the Abbottabad, Pakistan residence.

In none of these cases was Biden's judgment the final word. As president, it is, and so it is important not only to consider his experience – successes and failures – but moreover the political and foreign policy values and goals derived from that experience. This chapter examines the foreign policy agenda Biden has laid out for himself and his administration. The agenda, as presented in public documents, will serve later in this book as the guideline for assessing Biden's accomplishments in the early stages of his administration and, perhaps more importantly, the potential for and obstacles to success in meeting those goals during the remainder of his presidency.

Restoring American leadership: Biden's prime objective

There perhaps was no more important general goal articulated by Biden during the campaign and after winning the presidency than restoring the position of the United States in the world as a principled, responsible leader and model democracy. Standing in stark contrast to Trump's dismissal of international leadership as too costly and not worth his time, Biden's much more traditional view of the U.S. role in the world led him in the direct opposite direction. During the campaign, Biden criticized how Trump "belittled, undermined, and in some cases abandoned U.S. allies and partners."[10] He intended to reverse that course, starting with rebuilding strained alliances, and restoring cooperative ties with U.S. allies and partners. In his first major foreign policy speech as president, Biden pledged, "We will repair alliances and engage with the world once again…. We

---

9 Robert M. Gates, *Duty: Memoirs of a Secretary at War,* Alfred A. Knopf (New York: 2014).
10 "President-elect Biden on Foreign Policy," Council on Foreign Relations, November 7, 2020. https://www.cfr.org/election2020/candidate-tracker [accessed July 12, 2021].

will work with our partners to support restoration of democracy and the rule of law...."[11]

U.S. relations with its NATO allies and members of the European Union were at the heart of Biden's commitment, just as they were the main target for Trump's complaints. At the February 2021 Virtual Munich Security Conference, Biden promised his administration would "work closely with our European Union partners and the capitals across the continent – from Rome to Riga – to meet the range of shared challenges we face." He then deliberately responded to Trump's threat to abandon NATO, reaffirming America's steadfast commitment to its allies: "The United States is fully committed to our NATO Alliance, and I welcome Europe's growing investment in the military capabilities that enable our shared defense." Biden demonstrated America's return to international leadership by pledging to repair fractured ties, like those with Germany, and reenter agreements that Trump abandoned, like the Paris climate accord. Through numerous speeches and documents, Biden mounted his presidential agenda, laying the groundwork to regain global respect, trust, and confidence that had been diminished by Trump.

Diplomacy Rooted in Democracy: liberal democracy at home and abroad

As the key approach to rebuilding America's role in the world, Biden pledged to make diplomacy the leading tool of U.S. foreign policy, ahead of the threat or use of force. The diplomatic tool, Biden said, would be based on America's "most cherished democratic values", including "defending freedom, championing opportunity, upholding universal rights, respecting the rule of law, and treating every person with dignity."[12] A core component of this approach would be rebuilding the Department of State, which had been torn apart by the Trump administration. President Trump held the State department and professional diplomats in low regard, and his assault on traditional diplomacy led many of the best career officials to abandon their careers or, if eligible, retire from the Foreign Service.

---

11 "Remarks by President Biden on America's Place in the World," The White House, February 4, 2021. https://www.whitehouse.gov/briefing-room/speeches-remarks/2021/02/04/remarks-by-president-biden-on-americas-place-in-the-world/ [accessed July 12, 2021].
12 Ibid.

This aspect of Biden's approach recognized that authoritarianism and populism had recently made significant gains around the world and that the style and policies of the Trump administration had aided and abetted that tendency. According to Secretary of State Antony Blinken, four years of the Trump presidency allowed authoritarian governments to "seize every opportunity to sow doubts about the strength of our democracy."[13] To counter this growing threat, Biden pledged an active democracy promotion program. His approach recognized that both China and Russia were presenting alternative models for the international system; these models contrasted sharply with and challenged the model called "liberal international democracy," which the United States has led and promoted for decades. With the United States dropping active support for liberal democracy under Trump, the alternative models had developed increased attraction around the world, particularly with China's approach featuring trade and investment opportunities not linked to democratic values or human rights.

In Biden's speech to the 2021 Virtual Munich Security Conference, he called democracy promotion "our galvanizing mission" and declared, "Democracy doesn't happen by accident. We have to defend it, fight for it strengthen it, renew it. We have to prove that our model isn't a relic of our history; it's the single best way to revitalize the promise of our future."[14] Biden put the United States back in front of the world as the leading proponent of democracy, creating some high hurdles for his foreign policy team to surmount in his first term as president.

China: the leading nation-state challenger

One issue on which there was a degree of overlap between the Trump and Biden administrations was the perceived need to address the multiple challenges posed by China, an emerging global superpower. Those challenges were built on China's growing economic strength and the use of that strength to implement the Belt and Road, or new Silk Road, initiative through which China was expanding

---

13 Antony J. Blinken, "A Foreign Policy for the American People," Department of State, March 3, 2021. https://www.state.gov/a-foreign-policy-for-the-american-people/ [accessed July 17, 2021]. President elect .... op. cit.

14 "Remarks by President Biden at the 2021 Virtual Munich Security Conference," The White House, February 19, 2021. https://www.whitehouse.gov/briefing-room/speeches-remarks/2021/02/19/remarks-by-president-biden-at-the-2021-virtual-munich-security-conference/ [accessed July 13, 2021].

not only its financial and trade connections globally but also building its geostrategic presence around the world. Trump's abandonment of U.S. international leadership created vacuums around the world that China sought to fill, even in relations with key U.S. allies. For example, China has invested in a variety of businesses and infrastructure in several European countries, including purchases of Italian port facilities in Genoa and Trieste.

The "consensus" between the two administrations ended, however when it came to questions about how to defend American interests given the various challenges from China. During the Obama administration, Vice President Biden had been a supporter of the Trans-Pacific Partnership (TPP), which Trump abandoned early on in his administration. Biden came to office critical of how the Trump administration had managed the sanctions against China, as well as U.S. participation in the TPP.

He called Trump's tariffs against China "erratic" and "self-defeating," in part because they had cost American farmers important sales to the Chinese market, losses for which the administration was forced to compensate the farmers. Biden advocated for a "targeted retaliation against China using existing trade laws and building a united front of allies."[15] Having put the framework for multilateral cooperation with partners and allies in place, Biden said the United States would increase its naval presence in the Asia-Pacific and deepen ties with Australia, Indonesia, Japan, and South Korea. He also called for China to be held to the international economic and moral standards, urging the "free world" to unite against its "high-tech authoritarianism" and collectively push back against Chinese economic coercion. Biden reestablished the United States as a champion of democratic values by introducing human rights into the equation: he deemed China's inhumane treatment of Muslims in the Xinjiang region "unconscionable," and supported sanctions targeted against those involved.

However, the proposed approach was not entirely confrontational, as Biden said he was willing to work with China on issues like climate change and nuclear weapons control. But he called on U.S. allies in Europe and Asia to work with the United States to defend shared values and interests in the Pacific region. The net effect of the Biden approach was to cooperate where possible, confront when necessary.

---

15 President elect... op. cit.

Russia: defense, deterrence, and careful cooperation

Russia, of course, is a policy area where Biden also had a good bit of experience in his Senate career and then as Vice President. The contrast in approach with that of Trump could hardly have been sharper. While Trump was unwilling to criticize President Putin or Russia and even said in his 2017 summit meeting with Putin in Helsinki that he believed Putin over the judgment of his own intelligence community, Biden took a more traditional approach. He couched his Russia policy inside the commitment to diplomacy, saying he would engage Russia diplomatically when it best served U.S. interests and protected American security. But he also promised to confront Russia when necessary, including responses to cyber threats and attacks, election interference, and aggressive regional behavior, such as Russia's constant attacks on Ukraine.

In Biden's approach, arms control falls clearly in the realm of desirable cooperation with Russia, including the goal of negotiating a new strategic arms control agreement. But he opposed Trump's advocacy of readmitting Russia into the Group of Seven and supported working with European allies to sanction Russia for aggressive behaviors. He also specified Russia as one of the main external threats to Western democratic systems. In his Munich address, Biden judged that "Putin seeks to weaken the European project and our NATO Alliance. He wants to undermine the transatlantic unity and our resolve, because it's so much easier for the Kremlin to bully and threaten individual states than it is to negotiate with a strong and closely united transatlantic community."[16] He noted that challenges posed by "Russian recklessness" might be different than those with China, but that they were just as concerning. He identified defense of the sovereignty and territorial integrity of Ukraine as a "vital concern" for the United States and its European allies.

The bottom line for Biden regarding Russia is very much like the approach taken by NATO toward the Soviet Union in the Cold War: a combination of defense and détente, as outlined in the Harmel Doctrine. The alliance today is pursuing something like an updated Harmel approach that combines cooperation with defense and deterrence. Biden's policy toward Russia falls comfortably into that framework, which may be no surprise given his well-established involvement in NATO issues.

---

16 Remarks at the 2021 Virtual Munich... op. cit.

North Korea: danger in a small package

Trump's approach to North Korea was based largely on the personal relationship he attempted to establish with North Korean dictator Kim Jong Un. The goals of American policy in the Trump administration and in Biden's apparent intentions have been to obtain denuclearization of the Korean peninsula. Previous American attempts to move toward this end had been unsuccessful, but Trump apparently believed that he could make a "deal" with Kim that his predecessors had been unable to consummate. The approach, which Biden categorized as mere "photo-ops," was singularly unsuccessful, as North Korea continued developing its nuclear capabilities, with delivery systems threatening not just regional countries like Japan but also, ultimately, the United States.

While Biden did not abandon the denuclearization goal, he fundamentally shifted tactics to a more "calibrated, practical approach."[17] No longer seeking to pursue unproductive personal diplomacy with Kim, Biden pledged to work closely with U.S. allies, including South Korea and Japan, to pressure North Korea to abandon its nuclear weapons programs. This shift in policy was very pronounced, particularly given that, while schmoozing with Kim, Trump was distancing the United States from its support for South Korea.

Biden's approach has been described as seeking a "golden mean" between Obama's policy of withholding engagement from North Korea until the country changed its behavior and Trump's posture of a grand bargain of total sanctions relief in return for denuclearization. The Biden approach reportedly will pursue the goal in an incremental manner, with negotiations largely behind the scenes and expectations kept modest.[18]

Iran, Middle East: a new focus

The Trump administration identified Iran as a leading threat to the United States and made it a key focus of its Middle East policy, abandoning the multilateral Joint Comprehensive Plan of Action (JCPOA) aimed at stalling Iran's acquisition

---

[17] Scott A. Snyder, "Biden's Policy Review Leaves North Korea Challenge In Limbo," Council on Foreign Relations, May 19, 2021. https://www.cfr.org/blog/bidens-policy-review-leaves-north-korea-challenge-limbo [accessed July 17, 2021].

[18] Robert Einhorn, "The rollout of the Biden administration's North Korea policy review leaves unanswered questions," The Brookings Institution, May 4, 2021. https://www.brookings.edu/blog/order-from-chaos/2021/05/04/the-rollout-of-the-biden-administrations-north-korea-policy-review-leaves-unanswered-questions/ [accessed July 14, 2021].

of nuclear weapons. As discussed in Chapter 1, Trump intensified the conflicted relationship with Iran and strengthened U.S. support for Saudi Arabia and Israel, Iran's two leading rivals in the region.

President Biden had supported negotiation of the JCPOA during the Obama administration, and he came to office pledging to return to efforts seeking to keep Iran from ever obtaining nuclear weapons. At the same time, he pledged to work closely with European partners and allies to address Iran's "destabilizing activities" in the Middle East.

Biden also renewed U.S. support for a two-state solution to the Israeli-Palestinian conflict, criticizing Trump's "unilateral approach" to the issue while also criticizing Palestinian leaders for glorifying violence. He also called on Israel to "stop settlement activity in the occupied territories and provide more aid to Gaza."[19]

The key aspects of Biden's recommended Middle Eastern policy were resuming a multilateral approach to the challenges posed by Iran, maintaining a close relationship with Israel but one less dependent on Prime Minister Netanyahu, and being more critical of Saudi human rights practices.

Afghanistan: intending to head for the exits

President Trump had continued the process of removing U.S. troops from Afghanistan which had been underway in the George Bush and Obama administrations. Biden came to office promising he would end "the forever wars" in Afghanistan and the Middle East.[20] He said he would return U.S. troops from Afghanistan during his first term and work with countries in the region to seek future protection of U.S. interests there.

Biden explained his approach acknowledging that he, along with a substantial majority in Congress, supported invading Afghanistan in 2001 with the objective of ensuring "Afghanistan would not be used as a base from which to attack our homeland again."[21] He argued that when the United States eliminated Osama bin Laden during the Obama administration, the original U.S. objectives had been fulfilled: "War in Afghanistan was never meant to be a multi-generational undertaking. We were attacked. We went to war with clear goals. We ach-

---

19 President elect... op. cit.
20 President elect.... op. cit.
21 "Remarks by President Biden on the Way Forward in Afghanistan," The White House, April 14, 2021. https://www.whitehouse.gov/briefing-room/speeches-remarks/2021/04/14/remarks-by-president-biden-on-the-way-forward-in-afghanistan/ [accessed July 17, 2021].

ieved those objectives.... And it's time to end this forever war." He announced the United States would begin withdrawing on May 1, 2021 – the date by which the Trump administration and the Taliban had agreed all U.S. troops would be withdrawn – and that they would be out by September 11, 2021. According to Biden, withdrawing troops would allow the United States to put greater focus on counterterrorism efforts as the terrorist threat has become more dispersed and "metastasized beyond Afghanistan."[22] The United States then could reorient and reorganize its counterterrorism posture to respond to these emerging threats in other regions like South Asia, Europe, the Middle East, and Africa.

Despite the military withdrawal, Biden pledged that the United States would maintain a diplomatic presence in Afghanistan by providing assistance to the Afghan National Defense and Security Forces (ANDSF), working with neighboring countries and allies, supporting the government, continuing civilian and humanitarian assistance, and speaking out for the rights of women and girls.

This firm commitment by Biden to withdraw troops seemed likely to generate controversy in some American circles, even though it was in many ways a continuation of policy already pursued by previous administrations. It would be hard for Republican opponents to criticize the decision but perhaps not as difficult for them to argue that the withdrawal was not being done effectively.

Cuba and Latin America: rejecting Trump unilateralism

The Trump administration reversed the historic decision by the Obama administration to open diplomatic and other ties with Cuba, a move that was strongly critiqued by the expatriate Cuban community in Florida. Candidate Biden pledged to return to the opening to Cuba and undo the sanctions that Trump had imposed on the communist regime in Havana. Biden insisted that the reopening would be dependent on commitments from the Cuban side, but that engaging with Cuba again would strengthen U.S. relations with Latin America and the Caribbean.[23]

As for the rest of Latin America, Biden argued that Trump had "taken a wrecking ball to our hemispheric ties."[24] He argued for reopening diplomatic ties not only with Cuba but also with Colombia and Panama. He also called Ven-

---

22 Remarks by President Biden on the Way Forward in Afghanistan, op. cit.
23 Jim DeFede, "Joe Biden Confident He'll Turn Florida Blue, Says He'll Restore Obama-Era Cuba Policies In Exclusive CBS4 Interview," April 27, 2020. https://miami.cbslocal.com/2020/04/27/cbs4-joe-biden-interview/ [accessed July 17, 2021].
24 President elect.... op. cit.

ezuelan President Nicolas Maduro a "tyrant" who should step down, calling for increased sanctions on the regime. At the same time, he argued for more aid to help Venezuela and neighboring countries deal with the refugee crisis that has been putting so much pressure on the southern border of the United States.

Consistent with Biden's approaches to other issues and regions, his Latin America foreign policy inclinations were founded in rejection of Trump's unilateralism and on the primacy of multilateral diplomacy.

Immigration: seeking more humane approach

Immigration is an issue that crosses over between domestic and foreign policy. In the Trump administration, it even became a national defense issue, with the president inventing the threat of refugee armies attacking America's southern border. The primary source of immigration issues is clearly Latin America, and while the Trump administration saw immigration as a challenge to defend the U.S. border, Biden came to office seeing it as requiring initiatives designed to get at the roots of the problem: the safety, economic, and humanitarian conditions in the Central American countries where thousands have been trying to escape for better lives in the United States.

Biden's immigration policy sought to restore American moral leadership on refugee issues. He proposed to do so, as his Secretary of State Antony Blinken said, by working "closely with other countries, especially our neighbors in Central America, to help them deliver better physical security and economic opportunity so people don't feel like migrating is the only way out and up."[25] Blinken pledged on behalf of President Biden that the administration would "work to create a humane and effective immigration system."

Biden's de-Trumping approach included increasing the number of refugee admissions, overturning the Muslim ban, and stopping the practice of separating children from their families at the border. He also supported granting citizenship to "Dreamers," undocumented children brought to America by their parents. This major set of changes obviously created policy challenges for the new administration – challenges that might prove difficult to overcome, at least in the near term.

---

25 A Foreign Policy for the American People, op. cit.

Counterterrorism: working with allies

Biden made a clear distinction between immigration issues and the threat of terrorism, particularly by removing the Muslim ban, which Trump had rationalized as necessary to minimize the number of would-be terrorists in the United States. Biden identified his strategy as "counterterrorism plus," designed to use small groups of U.S. special forces and aggressive air strikes to fight terrorist groups overseas rather than by large-scale troop deployments.[26]

In his presentation to the 2021 Virtual Munich Security Conference, Biden extended his goal of working more closely with allies to include locking down "fissile and radiological material to prevent terrorist groups from acquiring or using them."[27] Biden's intentions in fighting terrorism relied heavily on his broader goal of enhanced multilateral cooperation, particularly with America's closest allies.

Pandemic policy: top domestic priority influencing foreign policy

Dealing with the Covid-19 pandemic in the Trump administration initially featured a policy of denial until scientific fact and spiking death toll forced a more focused and effective approach, leading to almost miraculous progress toward production of vaccines to stem the tide. And then, Trump refused to give the federal government a central role in coordinating pandemic responses, leaving it to the states to compete for resources and equipment required to deal with the immense health threats. The main foreign policy aspects of Trump administration policy were to focus on China as responsible for the spread of the disease and to limit the response largely to dealing with Covid in the United States, with little regard for international cooperation. In fact, Trump's signature action internationally was to pull the United States and its funding from the World Health Organization, accusing it of having let China off the hook for the global pandemic.

The Biden plan was to produce a nationally coordinated approach to testing, vaccine production and distribution, and healthcare requirements. It continued to focus on the question of the origins of the pandemic – not letting China escape blame – but concentrated on the need to promote a global approach, help-

---

26 President elect... op. cit.
27 Remarks at the Virtual 2021 Munich... op. cit.

ing in particular more vulnerable, less wealthy, nations in their response. This approach also recognized the need to strengthen global health security through the right investments and transparency to become better equipped for future pandemics. On the institutional level, Biden said he would restore the White House National Security Council Directorate for Global Health Security and Biodefense within the National Security Council that Trump had dismantled in 2018. Before coming to office, this already suggested that Biden saw the need for national security responses to the pandemic as well as more effective national-level coordination.

Climate change: returning to the Paris Climate Accord

Another policy area with both foreign and domestic aspects is climate change. The Trump administration's main approach to this issue was to deny the problem and to cut U.S. participation in international efforts to coordinate the response. The most symbolic move of Trump's approach internationally was his withdrawal of the United States from the 2015 Paris Agreement on climate change negotiated during the Obama administration. For Biden, this was an area where diplomacy and international cooperation were absolutely essential. He pledged to rejoin the Paris agreement and to reestablish the United States as a leader in cutting emissions and developing clean energy. Investing in renewable energy would not only power a clean energy future, but it would also equip Americans to thrive in the growing global renewable energy market. As a candidate, he set the goal of achieving a carbon-free electricity sector by 2035 and an American economy with net-zero emissions by 2050. Candidate Biden pledged he "he would bar U.S foreign aid and financing for coal-fired power plants overseas, provide debt-relief for countries implementing green policies, and expand Group of Twenty efforts to reduce fossil fuel subsidies worldwide."[28]

The Biden approach on climate change was a leading symbol of his intent to restore American international leadership. With this commitment, his administration could start rebuilding America's soft power, setting an example that would likely encourage other countries to emulate and follow the U.S. lead, largely without coercion.

---

28 President elect... op. cit.

Domestic "soft power" issues: fighting U.S. drift toward authoritarianism

Going beyond the pandemic response and climate change, several domestic policy areas play into Biden's leading priority for the foreign policy of his administration: restoring international respect for the United States. Foreign perceptions of a United States drifting away from its democratic ideals and practices were clear (see Chapter 1). Biden and his foreign policy advisors understood well that rebuilding American soft power would depend on whether he was able to right the domestic American ship of state.

Perhaps the most important plank of this platform was fighting the American drift toward authoritarianism under President Trump. For candidate Biden, doing so would require a successful campaign in which he won the presidency decisively and without question as to the victory's legitimacy. In November 2020, this outcome emerged clearly from the national elections. Despite Donald Trump and the Republicans' "Big Lie" that Trump had won, all the courts in which the results were tested concluded that the election had been fairly contested and called for Biden. That was not to be the end of the story, but it was at least the beginning.

To complement this approach, Biden pledged that his administration would be more transparent than the Trump one had been, seeking to regain the trust of the American people. He also promised to hold himself "accountable" to the American people, always asking, "Are we delivering results for you?" More difficult to ensure, perhaps, was his pledge to bring back nonpartisanship to the government and to pursue policies that could win bipartisan support. The foreign policy element of this idea was that a more united country would be far more influential and respected internationally. Unity, of course, would require cooperation from the Republicans.

Another critical part of the Biden soft power agenda was to resume the march toward racial equity whose progress had stalled during the Trump presidency. He acknowledged systemic racism and pledged to address the racial wealth, opportunity, and jobs gaps for Black and Brown people. Part of his plan was to "empower small business creation and expansion in economically disadvantaged areas – and particularly for Black-, Latino-, AAPI-, and Native American-owned businesses."[29] The election and re-election of Barack Obama

---

[29] Joe Biden, "The Biden plan to build back better by advancing racial equity across the American economy," Biden-Harris Campaign, https://joebiden.com/racial-economic-equity/ [accessed July 18, 2021].

as president had enhanced America's image abroad, but the events during the Trump administration raised questions as to whether the United States had actually made as much progress as some thought.

In a related area, Biden pledged to defend and protect the equal rights of all people, regardless of skin color, religion, ethnicity, sexuality, and the like. After assuming the presidency, he made clear that defending equal rights of people was part of his foreign policy agenda but would depend for its legitimacy on how effectively equal rights were pursued at home. In his first major foreign policy speech as president, Biden proclaimed that by defending equal rights for people all over the world including "women and girls, LGBTQ individuals, indigenous communities, and people with disabilities- we also ensure that those rights are protected for own children here in America."[30]

Finally, Biden understood that all these objectives would require support from a solid economy that fortified American democracy, increased faith in the role of the national government, and enhanced American competitiveness abroad. That, he argued, would require investments at home to promote job creation and ensure all Americans share in the dividends. Additionally, investments abroad would "create new markets for our products and reduce the likelihood of instability, violence, and mass migrations."[31]

Foreign policy based on strong, united nation: Biden seeks bipartisanship

The bottom line is that Biden proposed to unite the nation behind the objectives of domestic well-being, equity, and security as the foundation for an American foreign policy that wins back the trust and confidence of allies while warning adversaries not to try to count on American decline. The Biden approach would rely not just on America's military establishment, the foundation for much of American "hard power," but also on the model presented to the world of a reliable democracy that was wise in using its still-substantial power as well as intent on working with allies, partners, and international organizations on behalf of shared goals. The point is clear: without a strong domestic foundation, it would be difficult to pursue the core Biden international objectives.

---

[30] Remarks by President Biden on America's Place in the World, op. cit.
[31] Ibid.

The next chapter provides an early assessment of how successful President Biden has been in working toward the foreign policy goals he set for himself and his administration.

Chapter 3
Biden's beginning a mixed bag

This chapter reports on Joe Biden's initial steps toward the goals identified in the previous chapter. Though not every action is included, the overview provided does represent the foundation on which Biden's attempt to bring America back will be constructed. This first look suggests that the mixed bag of results now documented could well indicate some of the areas of likely success and potential failures down the road.

Restoring American leadership: the right words

To some extent, restoring American leadership is based on Biden saying the right words, but it ultimately will depend on whether those words are followed by credible actions.

The initial reactions of U.S. allies, who are the most important potential followers of U.S. leadership, suggests a certain wariness – not directed at Biden's sincerity but based in questioning whether he will be successful in de-Trumping U.S. foreign policy. The fact that Trump's Republican party still looks to the ex-president for leadership and that he has remained an active political figure raises questions about whether Trumpism has been defeated or just put on a temporary hold. The threat of a Trump resurgence in 2024 may be the uncertainty about the United States that most worries much of the rest of the world.

European public opinion in the early months of the Biden presidency suffered from a Trump hangover, and questions about reliability still influence negative views of the United States in many NATO and European Union countries. As Biden prepared to leave on his inaugural presidential trip to Europe, a major opinion survey reflected skepticism regarding American leadership: "Several recent U.S. polls show Americans believe that Biden's presence in office for the past four months has already improved the country's image among its allies. But this latest survey of Europeans shows he's created no 'bounce' whatsoever."[32]

---

[32] Benjamin Fearnow, "Poll Shows US Image Problem in Europe Persists as Biden Embarks on Trip to Repair Ties," *Newsweek*, June 7, 2021. https://www.newsweek.com/poll-shows-us-image-problem-europe-persists-biden-embarks-trip-repair-ties-1598249 [accessed July 24, 2021].

https://doi.org/10.1515/9783110759433-006

Biden's trip to Europe, however, seemed to bring allied governments back into a more comfortable zone in dealing with the American superpower. Demonstrating his long experience in dealing with foreign leaders, Biden got along well with British Prime Minister Boris Johnson and avoided potential pitfalls in Franco-British differences over the British exit from the European Union (BREXIT) and its implications for Northern Ireland. Even though the trip was to Europe, it took on a global character with the meeting on the British coast of the G-7, which includes Japan as well as the leading transatlantic economic powers. Rather than continuing discussions about former President Trump's proposal to invite Russia to rejoin the group, the G7 summit focused on more pressing concerns, like dealing with Covid-19 and environmental issues. Biden claimed, "America is back," and French President Macron said, "I think it's great to have the U.S. president part of the club and very willing to cooperate."[33]

Biden then focused on relations with members of the European Union and the U.S. NATO commitment. Meetings with EU leadership did not result in any major breakthroughs, but absent were U.S. threats to the EU and its members, which was a welcome change to EU leaders. One expert nonetheless warned, "Don't underestimate the Trump years as a shock to the E.U. There is the shadow of his return and the E.U. will be left in the cold again. So the E.U. is more cautious in embracing U.S. demands."[34]

As for NATO, the allies worked a little further toward developing a common policy toward challenges posed by China, supported the withdrawal from Afghanistan, and agreed to begin preparations for a new NATO strategic concept – something that had been put off during the Trump years out of fear of a potentially disastrous outcome. President Biden went out of his way to demonstrate U.S. support for NATO, saying that the alliance's collective defense provision was a "sacred obligation" for the United States. Biden repeatedly emphasized his focus on the struggle between democracy and autocracy but encountered some allied concern about whether this rhetoric could lead to cold war-type relationships with both Russia and China.[35]

On balance, Biden succeeded on the European trip in reassuring European leaders that the United States was indeed "back" even if he did not convince ev-

---

[33] Ashley Parker, "'Part of the club': Biden relishes revival of alliances that Trump dismissed," *The Washington Post*, June 15, 2021. https://www.washingtonpost.com/politics/biden-club-allies/2021/06/15/5a2fb206-cdad-11eb-9b7e-e06f6cfdece8_story.html [accessed July 24, 2021].

[34] Steven Erlanger, "Biden Is Embracing Europe, but Then What? NATO and the E.U. Have Concerns," *The New York Times*, June 6, 2021. https://www.nytimes.com/2021/06/06/world/europe/biden-nato-eu-trump.html [accessed July 24, 2021].

[35] Ibid.

eryone that an eventual return to Trumpism was not lurking in the shadows of America's very partisan domestic politics. Biden therefore would return to the United States to try to solidify the domestic base that, in his own words, provided the essential foundation for U.S. foreign policy.

Diplomacy Rooted in Democracy: restoring relations with allies

Biden's assertion that the United States and its allies are in a struggle for the survival of democracy may not have sat comfortably with some European leaders, but it remained a core part of the new president's rhetoric. Biden and his advisors clearly saw the trip as a demonstration of the administration's core message of defense of democracy at home and abroad.

That objective undoubtedly was accomplished, even though some allied leaders might have felt uncomfortable with too antagonistic an approach to the two main challengers to the Western system of liberal democracy. On the other hand, some observers might have felt that, despite Biden's assurances, his administration's actions included some much more pragmatic and less philosophical elements. For example, supporters of Ukraine's inclusion in NATO as a way of protecting its still-vulnerable democracy from Russian assaults likely were not fully satisfied with the important support promised to Kyiv because it stopped well-short of a path toward membership. The subsequent U.S.-German agreement that blessed completion of the Nord Stream II natural gas pipeline from Russia to Germany could be seen, on the one hand, as effective diplomacy with Germany. But, on the other hand, the agreement could be viewed as giving in on a project that could increase Russian political as well as economic influence in the West.

Looking beyond Europe, Biden's decision to complete the withdrawal from Afghanistan could be – and has been – construed as abandonment of an important democratization project. Perceived failure to give strong support to protests in Cuba against its communist regime could also be seen as a failure. In another case, the threat to democracy in Tunisia in mid-2021 presented additional challenges, and the Biden administration initially appeared uncertain how to respond.[36]

---

36 Josh Rogin, "Biden must try harder to stop the coup in Tunisia," The Washington Post, July 27, 2021. https://www.washingtonpost.com/opinions/2021/07/26/biden-act-coup-tunisia-democracy/ [accessed July 27, 2021].

The fact is that the opening period of the Biden regime has successfully demonstrated that diplomacy can, and should, possess a strong value foundation but also that the real world occasionally requires pragmatism, cooperation with adversaries, and even concessions based on other elements that determine national interests. Students of the "realist" school of foreign policy will affirm such an observation, even if politicians find it difficult to acknowledge.

China: seeking multilateral support for hard line toward Beijing

When Biden talked to European audiences about systemic challenges to the West's liberal democratic system, he was referring primarily to China and Russia. Both countries have suggested their models of interstate relations are superior to the Western one that has for decades dominated the international system. At the NATO summit, Biden sought agreement from the allies to create a democratic counterweight to Beijing's growing economic and military power. While the allies crafted a statement going beyond their December 2019 summit reference to the Chinese challenge, they generally preferred to be more cautious than the U.S. position was seeking. Future negotiations regarding a new NATO strategic concept will likely feature difficult negotiations on striking the right balance with regard to China.

Early in his presidency, Biden called Chinese leader Xi Jinping, reportedly pressing him hard on issues around the treatment of China's minority Muslim Uighur population in Xinjiang Province, China's threats against Taiwan, trade, and repression of democratic liberties in Hong Kong.[37] Although Biden has removed some of the hard-edged rhetoric from U.S. policy toward China and abandoned Trump's belief in his ability to make deals with dictators, U.S. policy has in many ways so far reflected some notable continuity with Trump's policies. The administration has taken some additional steps intended to limit diffusion of technology to China, but Xi warned Biden that bad relations between the two countries would be disastrous for both. Biden reported his response in a Tweet: "I told him I will work with China when it benefits the American people."[38]

---

[37] "US-China relations: Details released of Biden's first call with Xi," Reuters, February 11, 2021. https://www.bbc.com/news/world-56021205 [accessed July 24, 2021].
[38] Ibid.

The early Biden approach therefore included many aspects of his general approach to foreign policy. He has used diplomacy with allies to try to make U.S.-China policy more effective, seeking a coalition of democracies to balance China's growing power and influence. He has criticized China's human rights violations. His administration has sought to protect American industries, particularly from Chinese technology theft. Perhaps most significantly, he has used competition with China to fortify his argument that the United States needs to pour money into infrastructure, R&D in certain industries/technologies, universal pre-K education, improved health services, care for the elderly, and other government programs to prevent China from dominating technologies of the future. So, very particularly in policy toward China, Biden has identified strengthening the United States internally as a critical source of power and influence in dealing with China.

Whether the Biden model of conflict and cooperation with China will work for the Chinese was brought into question in meetings between Deputy Secretary of State Wendy R. Sherman and Chinese officials in July 2021. Following his meeting with Sherman, Chinese vice foreign minister Xie Feng reportedly said that the administration's policies are simply a "thinly veiled attempt to contain and suppress China."[39]

Russia: don't trust, do verify

Biden's first opportunity to put his Russia policy into practice came early in his presidency as he met with Russian President Vladimir Putin in Geneva on June 16, 2021. He did not go to the summit with any grand plan for resetting relations with Russia or achieving a breakthrough, but rather to establish a foundation for a more predictable, less troubled relationship with Russia. Biden's advisors said the President intended to establish some "guardrails" or "red lines" with Russia to reduce the times the United States would have to respond to aggressive Russian behaviors. In April, perhaps setting the tone for his meetings with Putin, he imposed sanctions on Russia, including blocking U.S. financial institutions from trading in Russian bonds. The moves were intended to respond to Russia's interference in the 2020 U.S. elections and the SolarWinds cyberattack, which had targeted U.S. government electronic networks and operators. Biden explicitly called

---

39 Chris Buckley and Steven Lee Myers, "Biden's China Strategy Meets Resistance at the Negotiating Table," *The New York Times*, July 26, 2021. https://www.nytimes.com/2021/07/26/world/asia/china-us-wendy-sherman.html?action=click&module=In%20Other%20News&pgtype=Homepage [accessed July 27, 2021].

out the Russian Foreign Intelligence Service as the sponsor of SolarWinds, making it clear to Putin that he knew the Russian attacks had high-level leadership support.

In Geneva, the two leaders reportedly exchanged complaints about the other's policies and actions but agreed to attempt to improve at least the channels of communication. The first step in this direction would be to renew the exchange of ambassadors – the Russian ambassador had been withdrawn in March after Biden had referred to Putin as a "killer." The Russians then asked the United States to withdraw its ambassador from Moscow. They also agreed to set up new dialogues on arms control limitations and discussed issues related to Iran, Syria, and Afghanistan.

Biden studiously avoided giving any appearance of a special relationship, learning from the mistakes of his predecessors – George Bush claiming he could see into Putin's soul, Obama being overheard telling Russian President Medvedev that he would have more flexibility to deal with relations after the 2012 elections, and Trump believing Putin more than U.S. intelligence agencies. Biden's strategy was, in that respect, successful, even though the meeting did not promise to put a lid on Russian meddling in American politics, stop Russian cyber attacks on U.S. private and governmental systems, or resolve any other of the issues troubling U.S.-Russian relations. As if to make his point that U.S. policy would be based on solid interest calculations, Biden said "You have to figure out what the other guy's self-interest is. Their self-interest. I don't trust anybody."[40]

North Korea: seeking contact, unsuccessfully

As in the case of Russia, Biden has avoided following in Trump's footsteps of praising and befriending North Korea's dictator Kim Jong-un. He has also followed through with his principle of working with allies, in this case by consulting actively with South Korea and Japan concerning the challenges posed by North Korea. Biden has kept in close touch with Japan's Prime Minister Suga. In April, the administration completed a month-long review of policy toward North Korea but provided little public information about its outcomes.

---

[40] Davie E. Sanger and Steven Erlanger, "For Biden, Europe Trip Achieved 2 Major Goals. And Then There Is Russia," The New York Times, Updated July 15, 2021. https://www.nytimes.com/2021/06/17/world/europe/joe-biden-vladimir-putin-usa-russia.html [accessed July 25, 2021].

As with the previous four administrations, Biden has set his goal as the complete denuclearization of the Korean peninsula, without necessarily believing that this can be accomplished in the near term. He is not seeking a grand bargain or relying simply on strategic patience. Instead, the Biden team is pursuing a calibrated approach that is open and willing to pursue diplomatic contacts with the Democratic People's Republic of Korea. North Korea turned a cold shoulder to the Biden administration suggestion of possible talks with the United States. Kim Yo-jong, the leader's sister and key spokesperson for the regime, commented somewhat vaguely, "It seems that the U.S. may interpret the situation in such a way as to seek a comfort for itself."[41] The question left for the administration was whether it would turn up the heat by resuming large-scale military exercises with South Korea or to keep that option in its back pocket as a possible response to North Korean resumption of nuclear or long-range missile testing.

Iran, Middle East: back to the nuclear deal

The Biden administration has not yet brought the United States back into the Joint Comprehensive Plan of Action (JCPOA) arrangement designed to stall Iran's development of nuclear weapons. The administration would like to get back on board but found itself at loggerheads with Iran, which wanted more punitive sanctions removed than the United States is willing to do before resuming negotiations. The United States argued that some of the sanctions were part of the JCPOA arrangement, not necessarily those added when Trump pulled the United States out.

In an area that greatly disappointed human rights advocates, the administration has not pushed Saudi Arabia on the murder of journalist Jamal Khashoggi, despite apparent evidence, confirmed by the intelligence community, that the order to kill came from the top of Saudi Arabia's regime. Some of the strongest concerns were expressed by members of Biden's own party, who believe Prince Mohammed bin Salman should be held accountable. Biden had called Saudi Arabia a "pariah" state with "no redeeming qualities" on the campaign trail but decided not to act when his national security team informed him there was no way to bar the prince from entering the United States or take legal pros-

---

41 Robbie Gramer, "Can Biden Solve the North Korea Puzzle? Biden opened the door for talks with Kim Jong Un, but Pyongyang is playing hard to get," *Foreign Policy*, June 28, 2021. https://foreignpolicy.com/2021/06/28/biden-north-korea-kim-jong-un-nuclear-talks-diplomacy-fail-succeed/ [accessed July 26, 2021].

ecutorial action against him without breaching diplomatic relations with the country, a key ally in the Middle East. Biden obviously concluded the cost of losing Saudi cooperation on counterterrorism and confronting Iran was too high. The Biden administration denied giving the country a pass, as the U.S. has implemented restrictions on lower-level officials and penalized elite elements of the Saudi military, but most objective observers judged the decision was one of those pragmatism over principles choices that most administrations confront.

In July 2021, the administration continued its steps toward lowering the U.S. military profile in the region, agreeing with the government of Iraq to remove all U.S. combat troops from that country. The United States will retain a training and advisory role with Iraq's military, but will no longer have a combat mission. This step bringing the post-9/11 era to a close is consistent with Biden's other actions in the region and his assertion that the United States needs to "fight the battles for the next 20 years, not the last 20."[42]

Afghanistan: preparing to leave

Biden's Afghan policy actions also fit into the attempt to transition beyond the 9/11 era in U.S. foreign and security policy. As noted in Chapter 2, Biden pledged to remove U.S. combat troops from Afghanistan by September 11, 2021, and in July the Department of Defense announced that the withdrawal would be complete by the end of August.

While the military has saluted and said "yes, Sir," as it should, not all military leaders were comfortable with the decision. Most would agree with Biden that the U.S. mission there went well beyond the original post 9/11 goals, but there is an understandable sense of regret that so many U.S. soldiers (over 2,300) died in the campaign without establishing a stable government. Biden has pledged that the forces remaining in the general vicinity will be able to prevent a new threat to the United States being constructed by al-Qaeda, the Islamic State, or other terrorists. However, the administration has no satisfactory response to the danger that growing Taliban control of the country will eventually

---

[42] Anne Gearan, "Biden, pulling combat forces from Iraq, seeks to end the post-9/11 era," The Washington Post, July 26, 2021, https://www.washingtonpost.com/politics/biden-iraq-911-era/2021/07/25/619c8fe6-ecb1-11eb-97a0-a09d10181e36_story.html?utm_campaign=wp_politics_am&utm_medium=email&utm_source=newsletter&wpisrc=nl_politics&carta-url=https%3 A%2F%2Fs2.washingtonpost.com%2Fcar-ln-tr%2F343d379%2F60fe9ff79d2fda945a190b87%2F5af5daa19bbc0f225bccd808%2F9%2F51%2F60fe9ff79d2fda945a190b87 [accessed July 26, 2021].

threaten educational opportunities for young girls, professional careers for women, and even the lives of girls and women throughout the country.

Even though the withdrawal commitment can be traced back to the Bush administration, and was pursued by Trump, any negative consequences – whether arising from terrorist activity or human rights disasters – may be laid at this administration's door. The decision and its early implementation can therefore be seen as either a courageous move or a risky gamble, and the outcome could play a big role in the final grade for the Biden presidency's foreign policy.

Cuba and Latin America: frustrated with Cuban repression

Biden's approach to Latin America has been to some extent frustrated by developments in Cuba. The microwave attacks on American personnel around the world that damaged diplomats' brain tissues started in Havana in 2016, and therefore they are referred to as the "Havana syndrome." Now reports of similar attacks have come from locations as diverse as Washington, D.C. and Vienna, Austria. It is speculated that either China or Russia is behind the attacks, but the fact that they were first detected in Havana stuck Cuba with the association. Added to this, protests in Cuba against the communist regime have complicated Biden's desire to move back toward a more open relationship with Cuba. In fact, the administration was pushed to impose sanctions on Cuban government officials for their role in suppressing dissent.

Beyond Cuba, the new administration re-set policy toward immigration from Latin America, sending Vice President Kamala Harris to Central America to start shaping an approach designed to deal with the root causes of large migration flows to the United States. The policy is in its early stages of development and will require congressional cooperation to dedicate foreign assistance to the countries that have been providing most of those seeking entry to the United States at its Southern border. Perhaps in part because of immigration being such a hot button issue in the United States, Harris spoke sternly to those who might be thinking of making the trip to the border: "Do not come," she warned, "You will be turned back." She also cautioned that the journey would be "a very treacherous and dangerous trek," a fact that has been demonstrated repeatedly over the years.[43]

---

43 Cleve R. Wootsen, Jr., "Harris wraps up a Latin America trip that featured sharp words to would-be immigrants," *The Washington Post*, June 8, 2021. https://www.washingtonpost.com/politics/kamala-harris-latin-america-trip/2021/06/08/279e360e-c859-11eb-81b1-34796c7393af_story.html [accessed July 28, 2021].

Immigration: new policies, but dealing with a surge

In April 2021 Biden reneged on his campaign promise, which he had affirmed in February, to lift the refugee cap from Trump's 15,000 limit to 62,500 through the 2021 fiscal years, with the goal of reaching a 125,000-annual limit. His announcement that he would keep the limit at 15,000 for the time being was immediately met with loud protests from Democrats and refugee advocates. Those protests led him to return on May 3 to his original commitment.[44] The administration claimed that Biden's April statement had been misinterpreted, but the sequence of corrections demonstrated the political and technical complexities around the issue.

That said, Biden moved decisively on several immigration issues, using his presidential prerogatives to issue executive orders that:
— reversed the Muslim ban.
— halted construction of the border wall.
— reversed Trump's expansion of immigration enforcement.
— reversed family separation at the border and created a task force to plan reunification for families that had been separated.
— ensured that Central Americans have access to asylum in the United States.
— rescinded Trump's order that immigrants must repay the government if they receive public benefits.
— expanded the U.S. Refugee Admissions Program and rescinded Trump policies that limited immigrations and raised vetting requirements; and
— directed relevant agencies to ensure LGTBQ+ refugees are not being discriminated against.

The overall picture of Biden's accomplishments on immigration policy – despite some stops and starts – is one of rapid implementation of many of the changes on which he had based his campaign pledges. Some of those changes were controversial and some may run into implementation issues. Some will likely require actions by Congress to provide authorizations and funding for steps taken in executive orders. But Biden did, overall, move quickly and decisively.

---

44 Michael D. Shear and Zolan Kanno-Youngs, "In Another Reversal, Biden Raises Limit on Number of Refugees Allowed Into the U.S.," *The Washington Post*, May 3, 2021. https://www.nytimes.com/2021/05/03/us/politics/biden-refugee-limit.html [accessed July 28, 2021].

Counterterrorism: new challenges after Afghan withdrawal?

Perhaps the most important counterterrorism action taken by the new administration was to complete the troop withdrawal from Afghanistan. Biden claimed the United States would be able to find and eliminate future threats, even if they emerge with footprints on Afghan soil. Whether this turns out to be the case or not may be the best measure for success or failure of this Biden policy. He now owns the wreckage, even if it is deeply rooted in the three presidencies that preceded him.

Competing with the Afghan withdrawal for the most significant Biden administration actions so far on counterterrorism is the clear shift of focus from the Trump administration on external threats to give domestic counterterrorism at least equal priority. This reorientation might have happened in any case, as the intelligence community has in recent years shined a brighter light on radical domestic groups that use or plan to use violence to achieve their ends. But the January 6, 2021, terrorist insurrection mounted at the U.S. Capitol pushed the domestic focus even higher up on the agenda. This new consideration does not mean any diminished concern about foreign sources of terrorism, but it does mean that counterterrorist resources in the Biden administration are likely to be focused at least equally on foreign and domestic sources of terrorism.

Pandemic policy: administration's biggest early success

Biden's strategy for the pandemic was to deal aggressively with Covid-19 through an enhanced vaccination program and new emphasis on masking as part of the response. The new administration took the Trump pandemic response, already significant in its production of vaccines in record time, and then put it on steroids. The policy included a direct assault on the virus itself and programs intended to deal with many of the economic and financial consequences of a year's disruption of America's social and economic fabric (see below). Both strategies produced substantial results. The majority – albeit not all – of Americans moved quickly to get in line for the vaccines, and within a few months pandemic numbers headed down: infections, hospitalizations and deaths all dropped dramatically. However, resistance largely promoted by right wing commentators and politicians, including Fox News, brought vaccination progress to a crawl before the country had reached herd immunity. The anti-vaccine movement and the spread of misinformation brought the nation to a new situation described by many as a "pandemic of the unvaccinated," featuring the dangerous Delta variant. By July 2021 most new cases, hospitalizations, and deaths were from the pool of unvaccinated Americans. Only then did some anti-vaxxer politicians and commentators change their tune and started recommending vaccination.

The new surge in Covid infections pushed the Biden Administration toward reversing the easing of its masking recommendations, despite resistance from some parts of the country – most prominently "red" pro-Trump states – and segments of the population, including both politically-motivated anti-vaxxers and those with inadequate information about the threats posed by Covid and the relative safety of getting vaccinated.

From a foreign policy perspective, the domestic Biden approach won a degree of respect and potentially increased soft power from foreign observers and nations. But the relative success in fighting the virus and its consequences inside the United States stood in stark contrast to what was happening in much of the rest of the world. Even close U.S. allies found themselves losing out to the United States in competition to access initially finite vaccine supplies.[45] But once policy had moved things in the right directions in the United States, the new administration sought to develop that aspect of the anti-virus approach, renewing U.S. cooperation with the World Health Organization and starting to ship millions of doses of vaccine to countries in need.

As with so many other areas of foreign and domestic policy, the administration's success in dealing with the pandemic is partly beyond its control. To the extent that it has been able to provide an effective response, particularly with its rollout of the vaccines, it has been successful. On the other hand, to the extent that there are limits on the willingness of some jurisdictions and individuals to cooperate, the interim outcome was frustrating for the administration and the majority of Americans.

Climate change: building foundation for international cooperation

Regarding climate change policy, Biden responded decisively both to his domestic political base priorities and his campaign pledge to rejoin international cooperation in dealing with and other international challenges. After assuming the presidency, he acted swiftly to cancel the Keystone XL pipeline – an action en-

---

[45] Marlon González and Zeke Miller, "From scarcity to abundance: US faces calls to share vaccines.: Associated Press, April 24, 2021 https://apnews.com/article/health-business-government-and-politics-immigration-europe-f6875e3094b1a51e9e8fc8ee84529ef0 [accessed July 29, 2021].

vironmentalists had urged – and re-establish the presidential Council of Advisors on Science and Technology with a focus on science and the environment.

The leading symbol of the change from Trump to Biden was the United States rejoining the 2015 Paris Agreement on climate change. The first steps toward returning were warmly welcomed by allies and partners alike. Biden also demonstrated his intentions by producing a plan to cut greenhouse gas emission levels in half from 2005 levels within the next decade, aiming to reach as much as a 52% reduction by 2030. Biden announced the commitment at a two-day virtual climate summit of some 40 world leaders that he had organized to mark 2021 Earth Day. His message to fellow leaders, perhaps aimed as much at a domestic as a foreign audience, was that effective responses to climate change would produce new and better jobs and economic growth: "I see autoworkers building the next generation of electric vehicles. I see the engineers and the construction workers building new carbon capture and green hydrogen plants."[46]

Biden's original $2 trillion infrastructure plan had to be substantially modified and cut back to win enough Republican votes to make it through the Senate. But the plan still included Biden's desired focus on transition to clean energy. Thus, while the most committed of environmentalists in the Democratic Party may not be happy that Biden has not sought implementation of a "green new deal," he clearly has moved U.S. policies and priorities in that general direction and has done so while largely keeping much of American industrial leadership on board by demonstrating the opportunities for growth in which they can invest.

In sum, the early months of his presidency saw Biden pursue the path on climate change that had been suggested by his campaign. His approach has been responsive to the climate crisis, developed with hopes to gain both industrial and bipartisan political support, and consistent with a foreign policy that puts the United States back in a leading position on the issue.

Domestic "soft power" issues: "building back better"

As noted in Chapter 2, to rebuild American soft power abroad, Biden knew that he would have to, as his campaign suggested, "build back better." The first re-

---

[46] Scott Detrow and Nathan Rott, "At Biden Climate Summit, World Leaders Pledge To Do More, Act Faster,"
National Public Radio, Updated April 22, 2021. https://www.npr.org/2021/04/22/989491975/at-climate-summit-biden-stresses-u-s-commitment-and-economic-opportunity [accessed July 29, 2021].

quirement in this area was dealing with the pandemic and its consequences. The assault on the Covid virus has been discussed above, but the second part of the response had to deal with the financial, economic, and social challenges created by the pandemic. Biden's administration acted swiftly, some of the actions taken by the issuance of more executive orders in his first 100 days than any of the three previous presidents. But the bulk of the response would require congressional action to authorize and appropriate the funds required – and these amounts would not be trivial.

The Democrats won slim majorities in the House and Senate in the November election and subsequent run-offs, so slim in the Senate that they would need every Democratic senator to be on board to pass required legislation. The president would have preferred to find bipartisan answers to the big questions, but the Republicans, for the most part, adopted an uncooperative strategy, urged on by the defeated former president who not only claimed he had won the election but who insisted he was still the leader of the party and would make anyone who did not accept his leadership pay a political price. The party fell in line, forcing Biden and his congressional Democrats to pass the first big Covid response bill by a process called "reconciliation," requiring only a simple majority in the Senate, which the Democrats could produce with the tie-breaking vote of Vice President Harris.

The reconciliation process produced a massive Covid relief package that the Republicans criticized as "bloated" spending. It was three times the size of the most generous Republican counterproposal. The package that passed on March 11, 2021, included:

- $1,400 stimulus checks to individuals making up to $80,000, single parents earning $120,000 or less and couples with household incomes of no more than $160,000.
- $300 weekly unemployment insurance supplement until Labor Day.
- Increased child tax credits, $300 per child 5 and younger and $250 ages 6 to 17.
- Substantial, though temporary, expansion of healthcare subsidies.
- $130 billion to primary and secondary schools.
- $350 billion for local state and tribal governments.
- Support for small businesses and live performance venues.
- $28.6 billion in targeted restaurant relief.
- $30 billion for transit agencies.
- $10 billion for critical state infrastructure projects.
- $45 billion in rental, utility, and mortgage assistance.

The Republican opposition was not just based on the size of the package but also on its content. Some of the elements of the package were intended to be temporary, while others were clearly designed to be so attractive and essential that the GOP would have a difficult time turning them around. The package, combined with subsequent administration measures represented, as some judged, an expansion of the role of the federal government that could be compared with Franklin Delano Roosevelt's "New Deal" or Lyndon Johnson's "Great Society." One reporter observed, "In his first 100 days as president of the United States, Joe Biden has governed less like a chief executive whose party is clinging to the barest of majorities in the House and Senate, and more like a transformative figure with a broad public mandate for societal change."[47]

Despite Republican charges that Biden was leading the country into socialism, the capitalist system success indicators all suggested the opposite: a booming stock market, expanding employment, and a growing economy. The question became whether the Delta variant stage of the Covid pandemic combined with Republican obstruction would stall the progress being made.

At the same time, Biden was working on other promises he had made intended to strengthen American society by promoting greater equity and justice. Using executive orders in the early months of his presidency, Biden made some significant changes designed to implement his campaign pledges regarding various forms of discrimination.

On January 20, Biden rescinded Trump's 1776 Commission which had been packed with ideological conservatives, producing "a sweeping attack on liberal thought and activism that calls for a 'patriotic education,' defends America's founding against charges that it was tainted by slavery and likens progressivism to fascism."[48] A few days later he reversed the ban on transgender individuals serving in the military and strengthened compliance with the Fair Housing Act. He moved on several fronts to fight racial discrimination, including signing orders to:

— "direct the Department of Housing and Urban Development 'to take steps necessary to redress racially discriminatory federal housing policies';
— direct the Department of Justice to end its use of private prisons;

---

[47] Rob Garver, "With Massive Spending Plans, Biden Seeks to Remake Relationship Between Federal Government and Americans," Voice of America, April 29, 2021. https://www.voanews.com/usa/massive-spending-plans-biden-seeks-remake-relationship-between-federal-government-and-americans [accessed July 29, 2021].

[48] Michael Crowley and Jennifer Schuessler, "Trump's 1776 Commission Critiques Liberalism in Report Derided by Historians," *The New York Times*, updated January 20, 2021. https://www.nytimes.com/2021/01/18/us/politics/trump-1776-commission-report.html [accessed July 30, 2021].

- reaffirm the federal government's 'commitment to tribal sovereignty and consultation':
- and combat xenophobia against Asian American and Pacific Islanders."[49]

Actions in the early months of his presidency clearly demonstrated Biden's commitment to a vastly different approach to equity, justice, and discrimination than that taken by Trump. In this area, the new administration provided strong evidence of change that would enhance America's image and influence with allies and other democratic governments that valued the rule of law.

Foreign policy based on strong, united nation: it takes two to tango

If anything, the first months of the Biden administration moved the country away from, not closer to, a strong, united nation. While Biden personally continued to advocate national unity and bipartisan cooperation in dealing with the nation's issues, the political environment was anything but supportive. The underlying problem behind America's political polarization stemmed from the choice of the Republican party to switch from its traditional identity as the party of conservatives to the party of Trump. Throughout the country, many local GOP organizations remained led by Trump supporters and the media outlets most identified with Trump continued to be the main source of information for many of those supporters. In many states where Republicans controlled the legislature, new laws were promulgated, defended as intended to prevent "fraud" in future elections but which seemed designed to target voter access for populations most likely to vote Democratic. Promotion of the "big lie" that Trump had won the presidency and that Biden was not the legitimate president guaranteed that a significant minority of Americans would be basing their political choices on a wall of misinformation. Only a handful of Republicans, including most notably Representatives Liz Cheney and Adam Kinzinger, were willing to stand up against the lies being propagated by Trump and his supporters. Even the House minority leader, Representative Kevin McCarthy, who had initially blamed Trump for the January 6 insurrection, gave into Trump's demands for loyalty in support of the big lie.

---

[49] Brian Naylor, "Biden White House Aims To Advance Racial Equity With Executive Actions," *National Public Radio*, January 26, 2021. https://www.npr.org/sections/president-biden-takes-office/2021/01/26/960725707/biden-aims-to-advance-racial-equity-with-executive-actions [accessed July 30, 2021].

Biden realized some success in pursuit of bipartisan agreement on key legislative efforts, including legislation to fund infrastructure projects around the country. But to any foreign observer paying attention, the country still looked divided. Moreover, Trump's assertion of leadership and hints that he would seek the GOP candidacy for president in the 2024 elections rekindled foreign fears that the United States could easily be taken back to a Trump-style regime in four years. In the short term, foreign trust in the Biden administration's much more welcome approach was even qualified by the potential for the Republicans regaining control of the House and Senate in 2022. This reallocation of congressional seats would not necessarily change U.S. foreign policy directions now set by Biden, but it certainly would undermine his ability to "build America back better" and prepare the ground for a second term coming out of the 2024 elections.

The prospects for a strong and unified United States in the world at the end of the first seven months of the Biden administration looked hopeful on the one hand but a source of concern on the other. The next chapter looks in greater detail at the foreign and domestic obstacles that could derail Biden's attempt to de-Trump U.S. foreign policy and bring America back.

Chapter 4
What obstacles stand in Biden's way?

As we have already documented, President Biden's goal of bringing America back to a position of respect, influence and leadership internationally faces many obstacles. This chapter examines those potential impediments in detail and speculates on his chances of overcoming them. It examines the interaction between domestic politics in the United States and its international credibility and role.

Diplomacy Rooted in Democracy: restoring trust in U.S. model will not be easy

Biden's goal of promoting democracy was not only inspired by Trump's perceived threat to American democracy and his support for illiberal leaders abroad, but also by American traditions and, perhaps, myths. Democracy promotion as a core element of U.S. foreign policy depends not just on actions taken in relations with other states – sanctions against undemocratic behaviors, for example – but perhaps more importantly on the example set by the United States itself. One critically important source of American power for decades has been the role of American democracy as a model for the world. Fighting wars against dictators and, as victors, helping establish or re-establish democracy, has enhanced the perception that the United States can use its military strength and the power of its political model to protect and expand democracy around the globe.

World War II, when the United States and its allies defeated the axis powers led by Germany, Italy, and Japan, served as a source of pride for the United States and gave political credence to the belief that victory in a war against autocrats can result in the spread of democracy. Post-WWII Germany served as the leading case in point, where promotion of liberal democracy in the wake of Adolf Hitler's warlike dictatorship was confronted by the Soviet Union's spread of illiberal communist regimes to neighboring East European states. The United States responded to the Soviet ideological threat by helping post-war West Germany establish a democratic constitution ("Basic Law") and through Marshall Plan assistance, designed to help Germany and other European states recover from the war and build capitalist economic systems to carry the recoveries forward. The United States also joined other democracies in establishing a mutual defense alliance, NATO, "founded on the principles of democracy, individual liberty and the rule of law."

The relative success of these efforts created a persistent American belief that it could spread democracy with the combined use of its hard (coercion and payment) and soft (attraction without coercion, largely based on culture and political system) power, a combination that has come to be known as "smart power."[50] While smart power is in many cases an effective way for nations to accomplish their objectives, it is not a guarantee for democracy promotion. Perhaps the leading example to counter the post-WWII successes is that of the Vietnam War. The war was sold on anti-communist grounds and defended as a means of establishing a democratic, pro-Western, government in South Vietnam. The war completely failed to accomplish this democratic objective, despite great loss of American lives and expenditures. Somehow, however, it did not completely extinguish the belief that using military force combined with democracy promotion can stabilize other nations. That faulty premise served as part of the justification for remaining in Afghanistan long after the immediate goal of the campaign – eradication of the terrorist threat that had produced the 9/11 attacks – had been accomplished. Biden in fact abandoned that goal when he finalized the troop withdrawal, without necessarily accounting for the implications it held for his democracy objectives.

If Biden's democracy objectives grew out of American tradition, or myths, they also were stimulated by international pressures leading away from liberal democracy. With an autocratic Trump occupying the White House, illiberal leaders abroad were encouraged to believe that the United States no longer presented the best governance model for their nations. The threat of radical right populist politicians and political parties to democratic governance grew in the absence of a strong beacon of democracy emanating from the United States. Even East European countries that had been admitted to NATO as "new democracies," including notably Hungary and Poland, moved toward more illiberal applications of political control. Turkey, the NATO member that had been touted as the only Islamic majority democratic nation, was moved decisively toward illiberal governance by President Recep Tayyip Erdoğan. These are just a few examples revealing the developing impatience with Western-style liberal democracy and growing temptations to accept some other, less democratic, and more autocratic approaches to governance. Thus, the Biden democracy goal was influenced by

---

50 Doug Gavel, "Joseph Nye on Smart Power," Interview with Joe Nye, *Harvard Kennedy School Insight*, July 3, 2008. https://www.belfercenter.org/publication/joseph-nye-smart-power [accessed August 1, 2021].

threats to as well as hopes for the future of liberal democracy, practiced within the rule of law.[51]

Any hopes Biden might have entertained that his decisive victory over Donald Trump in the November 2020 election would turn the country away from the illiberal directions Trump was taking were called into question on January 6. On that day, a joint session of Congress was scheduled to count electoral votes by state and confirm the outcome of the presidential election. That morning, Trump held a rally down the street from Capitol Hill claiming the election had been stolen and encouraging his supporters to march on the Capitol. The extent to which Trump was complicit in the violent insurrection that followed remains to be determined, but there was no question insurrectionists had been incited by the President, believed his "big lie," and judged the scene as a call to use force to stop the process of constitutionally validating Biden's victory.

In fact, the events of January 6 most likely crystalized the intimate connections between the health of American democracy and the ability to promote democracy abroad for the Biden administration. For the time being, it represented a setback to the extent it demonstrated the fragility of the American model. At the same time, the insurrection provided even more incentive to make the defense of liberal democracy a core element of his foreign and domestic agenda.

Commentator Fareed Zakaria has observed[52] that preserving a liberal democratic system requires constant attention and adaptation. Basing his analysis on a book[53] by two scholars, Daron Acemoglu and James A. Robinson, he has argued that liberal democracy functions in a "narrow corridor." Zakaria writes "Liberal democracy is the Goldilocks form of government. It needs a state that is strong enough to govern effectively but not so strong that it crushes the liberties and rights of its people." The not too hot (strength and stability of the state), and not too cold (protecting rights via civil society), but just right, is a difficult balance to maintain. Circumstances around this corridor are constantly in flux, and the balance faces challenges from the left and the right. Zakaria points out that deep divisions in American society, revealed dramatically by the January 6

---

[51] For a detailed examination of the challenges posed by these tendencies, see: Stanley R. Sloan, *Transatlantic Traumas: Has illiberalism brought the West to the brink of collapse?* Manchester University Press: 2018.
[52] Fareed Zakaria, "The narrow path to liberal democracy," *The Washington Post*, July 29, 2021. https://www.washingtonpost.com/opinions/2021/07/29/world-is-reminding-us-that-democracy-is-hard/ [accessed August 2, 2021].
[53] Daron Acemoglu and James A. Robinson, *The Narrow Corridor: States, Societies, and the Fate of Liberty*, New York: Penguin Books, 2019.

insurrection, are straining American political institutions – the guardrails preserving the corridor. Biden is being forced to pursue his democracy objective in this tense and, in many ways, perilous environment.

Meanwhile, European populist radical right parties may have been weakened by their failure to respond effectively to the pandemic,[54] but the right remains in control in Hungary and Poland. Moreover, a centerpiece of the so-called Arab Spring was the revolution that began late in 2010, leading to the establishment of a democratic system in the North African state of Tunisia the following year. In the first half of 2021, that progress was obstructed when the democratically elected president, Kais Saied, fired the prime minister, suspended parliament, and took full control of the government. He imposed strict limits on protests and public gatherings in general, provoking charges by his opponents that he had carried out a coup, overthrowing the democratic government and replacing it with an authoritarian regime, led solely by Saied. A *New York Times* reporter covering the whole affair was struck by the fact that most average citizens she interviewed in the capital of Tunis seemed unconcerned about the fact that the only Arab Spring democracy that had lasted until 2021 had been trashed. She observed, "People seemed content to wait and see what the man they had entrusted with their country would do to fix it. You had to wonder whether democracy the way the West sees it was what many of them had wanted in the first place, or just to live better, with dignity and more freedoms."[55]

The Tunisian case at the very least once again calls into question whether the United States can deploy U.S. foreign policy with sufficient influence to affect the course of internal developments in other countries. History and contemporary developments suggest that deploying diplomacy based on democracy is a bridge too far, and perhaps the United States should aim somewhat lower. Defending democracy where it is already in place and being more realistic about the difficulties of establishing democracy where it does not have its own internal roots may be a better combination. Such an approach might win greater trust in allied states and respect for America's use of its power in adversarial states. Whether Biden's approach to basing its diplomacy on democracy will move in such directions remains to be seen.

---

54 Bojan Pancevski, "Why the Covid-19 Pandemic Weakened Far-Right Groups in Europe," *The Wall Street Journal*, June 30, 2021. https://www.wsj.com/articles/why-the-covid-19-pandemic-weakened-far-right-groups-in-europe-11625054400 [accessed August 12, 2021].
55 Vivian Yee, "Tunisia's President Holds Forth on Freedoms After Seizing Power," *The New York Times*, August 1, 2021. https://www.nytimes.com/2021/08/01/world/middleeast/tunisia-president-kais-saied.html?smid=tw-share [accessed August 12, 2021].

Finally, one structural problem confronting Biden's democracy diplomacy is that he inherited a Department of State seriously weakened by the departure of many senior, experienced diplomats who were driven out by Trump's attacks on career civil servants and what he called the "deep state." Trump's assault on non-political government employees hurt many government agencies in terms of retaining experienced officials and attracting quality new employees. But his assault on the State Department, aided and abetted by his Secretaries of State Rex Tillerson and Mike Pompeo, was particularly devastating, and it will likely require more than one presidential term to repair the damage.[56]

China: presenting a competing model to liberal democracy

China is perhaps the most important nation-state obstacle standing in the path of Biden's attempt to "bring America back." Beijing is confronting the United States with a strategy that deploys military resources intended to challenge or balance those of the United States while attempting to offer a model of international leadership with diplomatic, military, economic, and financial resources designed to appeal to the interests of other states. Biden, in the first six months of his presidency, has maintained Trump's economic and trade sanctions, proposed massive infrastructure plans to boost American competitiveness, and formally charged China with genocide in the State Department's annual human rights report.[57] However, these measures do not respond fully to the long list of obstacles that threaten to block a successful Biden China policy.

Creating a united front of allies to collectively counter the Chinese threat stands at the forefront of Biden's policy agenda. Key partners include democratic nations in the Indo-Pacific, specifically Australia, India, South Korea, and Japan, as well as those in the European Union. With such countries valuing their close ties to the United States, and shared ideological values, Biden would certainly send a powerful response to China if he could promote a united front among key America's Asian and European allies. He found some success at his first NATO summit in June, managing to align allies on the belief that Beijing

---

[56] Ronan Farrow, "Can Biden Reverse Trump's Damage to the State Department?" *The New Yorker*, June 17, 2021. https://www.newyorker.com/books/page-turner/can-biden-reverse-trumps-damage-to-the-state-department [accessed August 12, 2021].

[57] Jonathan Tepperman, "Biden's Dangerous Doctrine," *Foreign Policy*, July 21, 2021. https://foreignpolicy.com/2021/07/21/bidens-china-doctrine-decoupling-cold-war/ [accessed August 5, 2021].

poses "systemic challenges" to global security and the international system.[58] The statement was a good start, but getting these nations to act in concert will not be easy.

China has positioned itself as one of the world's most important trading partners. Most of the countries that the United States needs support from, especially in the E.U. and Asia, have economies deeply intertwined with that of China. A decoupling strategy would be catastrophic for them. Although these nations share U.S. concerns regarding human rights violations, economic bullying, and military aggression, the stakes involved in potentially losing China as an economic partner are high enough to force them to move carefully toward any confrontational approach. But Biden will not be able to mount a coordinated, tough-line approach without allied support. The allies, therefore, face a difficult choice, and the Biden administration most likely will have to avoid pushing key allies toward making a stark choice between a tough U.S. line and their important financial and economic relationships with China.

While China continues to expand its economic influence, particularly through the Belt and Road policy, it also poses significant military challenges. Biden came to office pledging to maintain a strong naval presence in the Indo-Pacific, but China's disruptive behavior impedes that path. Since WWII, the principle of freedom of the seas has been firmly cemented as a universal pillar in international law. However, China has been active in the territorially disputed South China Sea, East China Sea, and Yellow Sea, undertaking island-building, military facility construction, and the transportation of military personnel and equipment. Because of the geostrategic significance of these bodies of water, the United States maintains a complex security framework with allies in Japan, South Korea, and the Philippines, and other security obligations to Taiwan, Vietnam, and Indonesia.[59] Maintaining a dominant stance in these regions would not only improve China's economic and military capabilities – controlling oil and gas activities, coercing neighboring countries, blockading Taiwan, and expanding its influence in the Western Pacific – but it would also limit the ability of the United States to uphold its security pledges and maintain stability in the

---

58 "NATO designates China a 'systemic' challenge," *Nikkei Asia*, June 15, 2021. https://asia.nikkei.com/Politics/International-relations/US-China-tensions/NATO-designates-China-a-systemic-challenge [accessed August 5, 2021].
59 "U.S.-China Strategic Competition in South and East China Seas: Background and Issues for Congress," Congressional Research Service, August 4, 2021. https://fas.org/sgp/crs/row/R42784.pdf [accessed August 5, 2021].

Western Pacific.[60] A constrained United States could produce wavering trust in its defense capabilities as well as a blow to international law.

Meanwhile, China holds in its hands the potential for causing a major issue with the United States if it steps up its campaign to bring Taiwan under the Chinese communist umbrella. Chinese governance in Hong Kong has demonstrated that individual liberty and democracy are threatening to the Chinese model of control. The security of Taiwan has been a hot button issue in American politics for decades. If the Chinese decide to push that button, Biden could be faced with a choice between acceding to Chinese demands or helping Taiwan defend itself, which could be a dangerous and costly deterrence and defense commitment. This risky proposition is why Biden will likely continue to caution China firmly concerning its aggressive behaviors that could produce military confrontations.

Despite his relatively stern rhetorical approach to China, Biden is willing to and believes he will be able to work with Beijing on shared challenges. However, if the Biden administration continues a hardline strategy, mistrust and dishonesty between the two global superpowers will continue to spike. Bilateral disagreements could mean that ideas for cooperation might never convert into joint actions. For example, an important step in strengthening current and future global health security involves determining the origin of Covid-19. Even with Biden doing his part in returning to the WHO, China continues to be slow in providing information like the genetic map or transmission rate of the virus.[61]

As an economic, military, financial, and diplomatic powerhouse, China is attempting to drive the international system of democracy toward a transactional world of autocracy. Hong Kong, a free society under the "one country, two systems" arrangement, suffers from police brutality, censorship, and a crackdown on pro-democracy protests. In Xinjiang, China has detained over one million Uyghurs, a Muslim minority group. According to detainees who have managed to escape, the internment camps, or the "re-education" camps as China calls them, force Uyghurs to study Marxism, pledge loyalty to the Chinese Communist Party, renounce Islam, and learn Mandarin.[62] The conditions in the camp are harsh, and prisoners suffer from heavy surveillance, sexual abuse, sleep deprivation, and family separation, among other cruelties.[63]

---

60 Ibid.
61 Ibid.
62 Lindsay Maizland, "China's Repression of Uyghurs in Xinjiang," Council on Foreign Relations, March 1, 2021. https://www.cfr.org/backgrounder/chinas-repression-uyghurs-xinjiang [accessed August 6,2021].
63 Ibid.

The Chinese government's disregard for human rights norms and international law despite widespread denunciation of its campaign against the Uyghurs is a frightening reality; as China becomes more globally integrated and a powerful voice at the international table, it can use tactics that leave a repressive blueprint on political and civic agendas around the world. Biden's human rights policy not only must check human rights abuses within Chinese borders, but it also must preserve the credibility of Western values to prevent Chinese authoritarian values from transforming the international system. However, framing of the U.S.-China clash as an ideological conflict also emboldens China to strengthen its side of the coin – authoritarian capitalism – while weakening its competitor – liberalism.[64] This conflict puts the global order at risk with the looming threat of illiberal leaders, democratic election interferences, and cyber and military threats. It seems that every one of Biden's China policy options has a long list of confounding issues to accompany its hopeful logic.

Overall, the Chinese challenge places obstacles in nearly every aspect of foreign policy as its pervasive economic foothold forces nations to make choices that balance their interests between a longstanding reliable partner in Washington and a growing economic partner in Beijing. In the end, the ability of the United States and its allies to find compromises to help shape common approaches to China may overcome many of the obstacles. "Compromise," according to Biden, is not a dirty word. But effective diplomacy will be required, particularly on the part of the United States, but also from Asian and European allies.

Russia: still actively interfering in Western democracies

Russia also offers an alternative international leadership to challenge that of the United States, and therefore of President Biden's goals for U.S. foreign policy. Russia has some very strong sources of coercive power, including its strategic nuclear forces, the excess of conventional military forces in the European area, energy resources that can be offered and then turned off, and impressive cyber-attack and misinformation potential. As for non-military power sources, it comes up much short of China. Moscow has the potential for influencing international perspectives on some issues including European and regional security, arms control, and energy. But its impact is often limited by suspicions of its intentions.

As discussed in Chapter 3, President Biden's strategic approach to Russia centers on keeping expectations modest, with the goal of establishing a more sta-

---

64 U.S.-China Strategic Competition... op cit.

ble relationship with Moscow and reducing the amount of time and energy the United States expends responding to Russian aggressions rather than of achieving friendly or cooperative relations.

One major obstacle to reducing tensions with Russia revolves around Ukraine. In April 2021, Russia amassed tens of thousands of troops at the border with Ukraine, exceeding the levels deployed when conflict first broke out in 2014.[65] Biden responded by delivering $275 million in military aid to Ukraine, and held another $100 million in reserve to respond to possible future Russian threatening acts.[66] Russia's military presence in and around Ukraine shows no sign of retreat, leaving Ukraine and the United States concerned that Russia could rapidly initiate a new offensive against Ukraine. Though Biden wishes to maintain stable and predictable relations, whether Russia will allow such stability by refraining from further action against Ukraine is mostly out of Biden's control.

Another roadblock in Biden's Russia policy arises in the form of Nord Stream 2, a natural gas pipeline under construction between Russia and Germany. A State Department spokesperson had sharply criticized the pipeline, calling it a "geopolitical project that threatens European energy security and undermines the security of Ukraine and eastern flank NATO Allies and partners," but the Biden administration made a deal with Germany in late July 2021 approving the completion of the project in return for Germany's agreement to take steps to mitigate potential threats to European energy security, to Ukraine, and to other EU and NATO member countries close to Russian borders.[67] The deal engendered a rebuke from Senate Foreign Relations Committee Chairman Robert Menendez as well as the chairs of the Foreign Affairs Committees in Estonia, Czech Republic, Ireland, Latvia, Poland, Ukraine, the United Kingdom, and Lithuania, who together released a joint statement stating that the completion of Nord Steam 2 "will strengthen the impact of Russian gas in the European energy mix, endanger the national security of EU member states and the United States,

---

[65] Amy Mackinnon, "Russia Further Ramps up Military Pressure on Ukraine," *Foreign Affairs*, April 2021. https://foreignpolicy.com/2021/04/20/russia-ukraine-black-sea-nato-biden-putin-zelensky-military/ [accessed August 12, 2021].

[66] Tony Czuczka, "U.S. Has More Ukraine Military Aid in Reserve, Biden Aide Says," Bloomberg, June 20, 2021. https://www.bloomberg.com/news/articles/2021-06-20/u-s-has-more-ukraine-military-aid-in-reserve-biden-aide-says [accessed August 12, 2021].

[67] Nicole Gaouette and Jennifer Hansler, "US and Germany reach deal on controversial pipeline that Biden sees as a Russian 'geopolitical project'," *CNN Politics*, July 21, 2021. https://www.cnn.com/2021/07/21/politics/us-german-nord-stream-2-deal/index.html [accessed August 12, 2021].

and threaten the already precarious security and sovereignty of Ukraine."[68] Such concerns arise from past examples of Russia cutting of energy supplies to Ukraine and other countries in an effort to undermine their governments and increase Russian influence.

In developing the U.S. position on Nord Stream 2, Biden was forced to weigh the path of undermining relations with Germany, as the German government supported the project and categorized it as a purely commercial endeavor, against angering bipartisan domestic forces as well as other European NATO allies who vehemently oppose the pipeline. Ultimately, Biden determined that fighting with Germany on the nearly complete pipeline would be a lost cause: "The idea that anything was going to be said or done [that could] stop it was not possible," he said.[69] It remains to be seen whether this choice was the right one, as serious repercussions for the hoped-for stability in U.S.-Russia relations could arise if Russia *does* eventually take advantage of the pipeline to threaten Ukraine both economically, as the Ukrainian government relies on natural gas as a major source of revenue, and politically, as Russian-back separatist forces still confront those of Ukraine.

Establishing a stable relationship with Russia is further challenged by the continuing threat of Kremlin-backed cyber-attacks on the United States and its allies. During their meeting in Geneva on June 16, 2021, Biden asked Putin to help the United States thwart criminal hackers working in Russia who have targeted American businesses and other institutions, but less than a month later the United States detected two more cyber-attacks from within Russia. One involved Russian hackers breaking into computers used by a contractor for the Republican National Committee, while the other was a ransomware attack affecting an estimated 1,500 businesses both in and outside of the United States.[70] Though the Biden administration reported progress on cyber security negotiations following the Geneva meeting and even agreed to set up meetings between senior cyber security experts in their governments to collaborate against criminal groups launching ransomware attacks from inside Russia, the fresh attacks in late June 2021 have cast doubt on whether Moscow is genuinely willing to take

---

68 Jennifer Hansler, "Top Democrat and European counterparts slam US-Germany deal on Nord Stream 2," *CNN Politics*, August 2, 2021. https://www.cnn.com/2021/08/02/politics/menendez-nord-stream-2-joint-statement/index.html [accessed August 12, 2021].
69 Ibid.
70 Brian Bennett, "Biden Administration Says Talks with Russia on Cyber Attacks Are Progressing. Privately, Staffers Are Skeptical," *Time*, July 8, 2021. https://time.com/6078997/biden-cyber-attacks-putin/ [accessed August 9, 2021].

action.[71] If continued negotiations with Russia on this issue fail to progress satisfactorily, President Biden may be forced to declare economic sanctions against Russia and launch offensive cyber-attacks against the criminals' networks. Of course, this course of action would work against the administration's efforts to establish a calmer relationship with Russia.

Likewise, nuclear arms control is a delicate issue for Biden to navigate in negotiations with Russia. The meeting at Geneva laid the groundwork for continuing bilateral talks on what the countries have termed "strategic stability," renewing the potential for cooperation between the two nuclear superpowers. However, major obstacles will need to be overcome to craft a mutually acceptable deal. A senior research fellow at the Center for Advanced American Studies at Moscow State Institute of International Relations noted, "Russia still has concerns with U.S. modification of heavy bombers and launchers to launch ballistic missiles, and that's been for a while now."[72] For its part, the Biden administration has criticized Russia's engagement in low-yield nuclear testing, which violates the nuclear testing moratorium.

Another persistent issue is the question of middle-range nuclear systems deployed in Europe. The United States and Russia agreed in 1987 to eliminate and permanently forswear all their medium range nuclear and conventional ground-launched ballistic and cruise missiles. In 2014, the United States began warning Russia that a new system it was developing would violate the 1987 treaty, but Russia carried on and began deploying the system in 2017. In 2019, the Trump administration withdrew from the treaty, after it had announced it would begin development of a new mobile middle range missile system of its own. The issue remains alive and could be yet another obstacle to Biden administration desires to re-energize arms control negotiations with Russia.

Lastly, Russia's internal authoritarianism and ongoing support for radical right parties and politicians throughout Europe – as well as for Trump in the United States – present direct challenges to the liberal democratic goals Biden has pledged the United States to represent and protect. There is no reason to believe that Moscow will suspend its support for Viktor Orban's increasingly autocratic government in Hungary or stop aiding radical right parties and politicians around Europe. On balance, Biden's election has been seen by the Kremlin as posing potential challenges to Russian national security because of Biden's proclaimed intentions to convene a summit of democracies to join forces against ris-

---

71 Ibid.
72 "US and Russia Hold Arms Control Talks in Geneva," *DW*, July 27, 2021. https://www.dw.com/en/us-and-russia-hold-arms-control-talks-in-geneva/a-58671440 [accessed August 9, 2021].

ing authoritarianism around the world. American support for democracy in post-Soviet countries like Belarus, Georgia, and Ukraine, all which Russia considers as within its security sphere, will likely continue to trouble U.S.-Russia relations. In Belarus especially, Putin has pledged economic and military support for Alexander Lukashenko following his contested (due to widespread allegations of vote-rigging) reelection in August 2020, while Biden has criticized Trump's silence over the Lukashenko regime's violent suppression of democratic activists.[73] Thus, Biden's goal of a less antagonistic relationship with Russia may be incompatible with his commitments to restoring democracy, particularly when applied to countries around Russia's periphery. And it might run head-long into future Russian meddling in American politics.

North Korea: small country presenting big problem

North Korea has the potential for creating vexing issues for the United States and for Biden's leadership aspirations. It presents absolutely no soft power challenge, as few nations or populations would aspire to emulate North Korea's form of government, status of individual liberties, or societal characteristics. But North Korea and its dictatorship led by Kim Jong-un have already developed nuclear weapons and delivery systems that are threats to the region and, increasingly, to the United States directly.

The first major barrier for Biden in dealing with North Korea lies in communication with a government that wraps itself in a dense cloak of secrecy. The Biden administration has reached out to Pyongyang through multiple channels to stimulate diplomatic efforts. However, a senior administration official has acknowledged that North Korea has been completely unresponsive to U.S. outreach following "over a year without active dialogue."[74] Kim Yo Jong, Kim Jong-un's sis-

---

[73] Tracey German, "Russia: Biden Brings a New US Challenge to Putin's Backyard," *The Conversation*, November 11, 2020. https://theconversation.com/russia-biden-brings-a-new-us-challenge-to-putins-backyard-149765 [accessed August 9, 2021].

[74] Arlette Saenz and Zachary Cohen, "Biden Administration started outreach to North Korea last month, but country is unresponsive," *CNN Politics*, March 13, 2021. https://www.cnn.com/2021/03/13/politics/north-korea-biden-administration-outreach/index.html [accessed August 7, 2021].

ter, warned that any assumption that North Korea seeks diplomacy with the United States could only lead to "a greater disappointment" down the line.[75]

Serious progress toward the U.S. goal of denuclearization of the Korean peninsula depends on constructive talks between the two countries, and North Korea's refusal to even respond prevents the Biden administration from working toward this goal. The deadlock could have several consequences. Given the uncooperative North Korean attitude toward previous U.S. administrations, North Korea may remain unwilling to give up its nuclear arsenal – valued as the heart of its security system and its primary deterrent against the United States and its ally South Korea. Trump's departure from the Iran nuclear deal may have convinced Kim that he could not trust the United States to remain committed to any nuclear deal with North Korea.[76] Even if Kim trusted Biden, he might wonder, as many international observers do, whether subsequent elections might bring Trump or someone of his ilk back to power. All these considerations suggest that American denuclearization objectives are likely to continue to face a skeptical and recalcitrant North Korean leadership.

For decades, U.S. Republican and Democratic administrations have imposed sanctions targeting North Korea's economy that have failed to stimulate progress on denuclearization talks. The Covid-19 pandemic, which led North Korea to seal its borders, has crippled the country's economy, apparently producing a far greater impact than previous U.S. sanctions. The Biden administration could rely on the pandemic to bring North Korea to a serious enough crisis to force Kim back to the table to try to open the way to assistance and sanctions relief. But this is not Kim's only option. North Korea has a history of making illicit trade deals with Middle Eastern countries, offering weapons in return for non-military necessities. Pyongyang might seek to strike deals with countries like Iran, Pakistan, and Syria. In theory, such deals could include nuclear weapons technology as well as missile sales with the potential to threaten regional stability and U.S. interests in the Middle East. A senior fellow at the Carnegie Endowment for International Peace puts the threat into perspective: "It is bad enough that Washington faces a complex nuclear challenge from North Korea in East Asia. But

---

[75] "Kim's sister says US interpreting signals from North Korea in 'wrong way,'" *Nikkei Asia*, June 23, 2021. https://asia.nikkei.com/Spotlight/N-Korea-at-crossroads/Kim-s-sister-says-US-interpreting-signals-from-North-Korea-in-wrong-way [accessed August 7, 2021].

[76] Doug Bandow, "What Happens if North Korea Won't Deal with Joe Biden?" CATO Institute, June 25, 2021. https://www.cato.org/commentary/what-happens-north-korea-wont-deal-joe-biden [accessed August 7, 2021].

North Korean proliferation that yields a new nuclear-armed state or catalyzes a wider conflict in the Middle East could be worse."[77]

The pressure is therefore on for the Biden administration to try to move Kim toward some form of constructive engagement with the United States. North Korea's economy, devastated by the convergence of the pandemic, sanctions, natural disasters, and its inherent weaknesses, present the administration with a unique opportunity to offer lifted sanctions and assistance in exchange for the beginning of a denuclearization process.

Toward this end, the United States would need to rely heavily on South Korea to help the North Korean economy while slowly integrating North Korea into the international system. But two obstacles confront the U.S.-South Korea relationship: Chinese interference and the impending South Korean presidential elections.[78] For years, China has attempted to deter cooperation between the two Koreas through economic coercion against South Korea while North Korea has sent conflicting messages to the United States and South Korea.[79] In addition, South Korean presidential elections are coming up in March of 2022. Although Biden and South Korean President Moon Jae-in have made progress developing common approaches to the North, the two administrations must work to establish a sense of continuity while garnering bipartisan support following any change in the South Korean government following the elections.[80]

Despite the apparently limited chances for serious progress toward denuclearization, the Biden administration has few options but to continue to try. The most fundamental block to progress, however, may be the fact that the Kim regime has little concern for and no accountability to its population. Years of oppression and brutal treatment of dissent have kept the regime in power, and the prospect of better conditions for the North Korean people may not outweigh the regime's concern for its own future.

---

[77] Toby Dalton, "The Most Urgent North Korean Nuclear Threat Isn't What You Think," Carnegie Endowment for International Peace, April 15, 2021. https://carnegieendowment.org/2021/04/15/most-urgent-north-korean-nuclear-threat-isn-t-what-you-think-pub-84335 [accessed August 7, 2021].

[78] Vincent Brooks and Ho Young Leem, "A Grand Bargain with North Korea," *Foreign Affairs*, July 29, 2021. https://www.foreignaffairs.com/articles/united-states/2021-07-29/grand-bargain-north-korea [accessed August 7, 2021].

[79] Ibid.

[80] Ibid.

Iran, Middle East: Biden needs Iran, Saudis, and Israel to cooperate

On the campaign trail, President Biden declared his intentions to smooth over relations with Iran and to rejoin the Joint Comprehensive Plan of Action (JCPOA) that was designed to suppress the Middle Eastern country's efforts toward nuclear weapons development. However, the Biden administration is finding it a major challenge to repair the damage done by Trump's 2018 withdrawal from the deal and his subsequent implementation of sanctions targeting hundreds of new targets and sectors in Iran (these sanctions being in addition to the reimplementation of sanctions that had been removed under the JCPOA). Rather than subduing Iran as Trump claimed severe sanctions would, the destruction of its domestic economy has done little to deter nuclear development, support for terrorism, or human rights abuses.[81] The United States has little leverage remaining to try to force Iran into a better or even the same deal, and the country's recent presidential election of conservative leader Ebrahim Raisi, who is likely to be less amenable to negotiations than his more moderate predecessor Hassan Rouhani, will likely only enhance the challenge. Discussions between the two sides have stagnated, making little progress as of August 2021 and clashing over prisoner swap negotiations in addition to other issues.[82] Neither side wants to move first, with Iran asking for sanction removal as a precondition and the United States demanding that compliance with JCPOA nuclear limits must come first.

Some other considerations complicating a return to the JCPOA include domestic opposition from politicians (mostly Republicans) who have consistently argued that the deal is too lenient and favorable for Iran, the reality that Iran has developed nuclear capabilities and technologies not accounted for in the original deal in the time between the 2018 nullification of the deal and Biden's attempts at reviving it, and unwillingness to push Iran from the countries who also signed the JCPOA (China, Germany, France, Russia, the United Kingdom, and Germany), most of whom were furious at the American withdrawal or, in the case of China and Russia, now are subject to their own sanctions from the

---

[81] Brian O'Toole, "Rejoining the Iran Nuclear Deal: Not so Easy," *Atlantic Council*, January 12, 2021, https://www.atlanticcouncil.org/in-depth-research-reports/issue-brief/rejoining-the-iran-nuclear-deal-not-so-easy/ [accessed August 9, 2021].

[82] Matthew Lee, "US Hits Iran for Delay in Nuclear and Prisoner Swap Talks," *AP News*, July 17, 2021, https://apnews.com/article/joe-biden-middle-east-government-and-politics-iran-iran-nuclear-d910911862e274c701af2fefcf20035e [accessed August 9, 2021].

United States. All in all, Biden has an incredibly difficult task in front of him if he wishes to convince Iran to comply with U.S. demands.

As for Saudi Arabia, the Biden administration appears to have decided to prioritize U.S. strategic interests in maintaining a friendly relationship with the Middle Eastern power and influential member in the Organization of Petroleum Exporting Countries (OPEC). Despite the revelation that Crown Prince Mohammed bin Salman had a direct role in the murder of journalist Jamal Khashoggi, the White House hosted the crown prince's brother Prince Khalid in July 2021 to discuss Saudi Arabia's cooperation in controlling the rise in oil prices with the goal of supporting the ongoing global economic recovery. According to a U.S. readout of National Security Advisor Jake Sullivan's conversation with Prince Khalid, Sullivan stressed the need to improve human rights in Saudi Arabia.[83] However, many critics consider the administration's lack of concrete action against the kingdom's blatant human rights abuses to be a major failure and contradiction to Biden's proclaimed commitment to upholding democratic ideals and guarding the universal rhetoric of human rights standards. The Biden position could stimulate more criticism down the road from his party's more liberal members whose support he needs because of the slim Democratic majorities in the Senate and House.

Regarding America's leading partner in the region, Israel, the path ahead for Biden may be somewhat eased by Prime Minister Netanyahu's election defeat and departure. But the new government, headed by Prime Minister Naftali Bennett, disagrees with the Biden approach to the JCPOA as well as on questions related to Israel-Palestinian relations, including settlement policy. The trick for Biden will be to pursue his policies while keeping disagreements with Israel confined to behind-the-scenes conversations. It seems that the Bennett government will likely accept the formula of agreeing to disagree while maintaining friendly bilateral relations and avoiding public dispute.

---

83 Ellen Knickmeyer, Matthew Lee, and Lolita Baldor, "US Hosts High-Level Saudi Visit after Khashoggi Killing," *AP News*, July 6. 2021, https://apnews.com/article/joe-biden-jamal-khashoggi-europe-middle-east-government-and-politics-fe49077941a4742da5dde3704d312927 [accessed August 9, 2021].

Afghanistan: Taliban takeover challenges Biden leadership goals

Many agree that Biden withdrawing troops from Afghanistan to end the "forever war" was a strategically wise decision that frees up American resources and personnel and allows for the administration to refocus efforts on other pressing foreign policy and defense challenges. However, the United States left behind a fatally fractured Afghanistan, vulnerable to Taliban rule and breeding grounds for terrorist groups. The potential for internal struggle remained with elements of the mujahideen in the north preparing to oppose the Taliban.[84] The fragile state of the country threatens a future that could challenge U.S. security and political interests as well as questioning American reliability in fulfilling its foreign commitments.

By mid-summer of 2021, the fall of Afghanistan to the Taliban became inevitable. Consequently, with no deployed U.S. or allied troop presence in Afghanistan, the ability to surveille and liquidate extremist groups became significantly reduced. For example, the American military and intelligence community has weakened al-Qaeda and the Islamic State, but the sudden withdrawal and Taliban takeover may give these groups greater freedom to regenerate activity against U.S. interests. An al-Qaeda resurgence poses serious risks to both the Afghan community and global security. Furthermore, no American troops on the ground makes air strikes particularly difficult. Launching an air strike from al-Udeid, the American air base outside Qatar, is the best option, but it is also the most expensive. The aerial refueling required by the fighter jets to travel to Afghanistan while also making sure to fly around Iran could strain the inventory. And gone are on-the-ground search-and-rescue backup missions and Joint Special Operations Command (JSOC) operatives to provide a security blanket for the air strikes.[85] Violence from al-Qaeda, the Islamic State, the Taliban, and other emerging insurgencies becomes an inevitable reality if the United States becomes unable to monitor and respond forcefully to threats.

The upsurge in Taliban attacks as the United States withdrew moved Afghanistan closer to a Taliban takeover of the entire country. The 2021 Annual Threat

---

84 Ahmad Massoud, "The mujahideen resistance to the Taliban begins now. But we need help," *The Washington Post*, August 18, 2021. https://www.washingtonpost.com/opinions/2021/08/18/mujahideen-resistance-taliban-ahmad-massoud/ [accessed August 18, 2021].
85 Missy Ryan, Shane Harris, and Paul Sonne, "After troops leave Afghanistan, U.S. will face challenges maintain counterterrorism capability, *The Washington Post*, April 17, 2021. https://www.washingtonpost.com/national-security/afghanistan-withdrawl-qaeda-us-counterterrorism/2021/04/17/4a383b46-9eb1-11eb-8a83-3bc1fa69c2e8_story.html [accessed August 9, 2021].

Assessment of the U.S. Intelligence Community detailed the "low prospects" of peace talks, the high probability that the Taliban will "make gains on the battlefield," and the struggle of the Afghan government to "hold recaptured territory or reestablish a presence in areas abandoned in 2020."[86] General Austin S. Miller declared that Taliban aggression paired with Afghan military defeat and psychological surrender could lead to an even greater conflict: "A civil war is certainly a path that can be visualized if this continues on the trajectory it's on right now."[87] But the quick victory for the Taliban might reduce the prospects for anything resembling a civil war, even though it could occasion massacres of government supporters and those who once worked for American forces and interests.

The United States spent nearly 20 years attempting to establish a stable non-Taliban government in Afghanistan, but that effort has been abandoned. The withdrawal of U.S. and allied forces, now complete, will free up resources for counterterrorism efforts and the ability to focus on pressing foreign policy areas like China. Although the consequences for Afghanistan and regional stability are grave, Biden obviously was willing to pay that price. The consequences for the Afghan people seem obvious: continuing civil conflict with substantial civilian deaths and displacements until the Taliban have brought the entire country under control. This new form of "stability" is not what the United States was seeking for two decades, but it now seems inevitable, along with severe consequences for issues like education and professional opportunities for women, which are likely to be constrained once again under the Taliban.

This result of the U.S. withdrawal was finally executed by Biden but was foreseen and substantially planned by the Bush, Obama, and Trump administrations. The final withdrawal has already stimulated an ongoing debate about the logic of the "forever war" now that it has been lost despite huge costs in Afghan, American and allied lives and expenditure of resources that could have gone to other important priorities. Although the decisions to support and then ultimately abandon the war were effectively taken by both U.S. political parties over many years, the Biden administration will be forced to offer the defenses and explanations of the final act and its consequences. The decision to withdraw was sup-

---

86 "Annual Threat Assessment of the US Intelligence Community," Office of the Director of National Intelligence, April 9, 2021. https://int.nyt.com/data/documenttools/annual-threat-assessment-report/5bd104278cd017bd/full.pdf [accessed August 9, 2021].
87 Kathy Gannon, "Top US general foresees Afghan civil war as security worsens," *AP News*, June 29, 2021. https://apnews.com/article/joe-biden-afghanistan-9636261069b03719d569b5cf9fe5e4e5 [accessed August 9, 2021].

ported by a majority of Americans,[88] but the humanitarian consequences could serve as a black mark on the administration's foreign policy record and raise new questions with allies about U.S. reliability. All of this could, at the least, distract from and even serve as an obstacle to the Biden democracy agenda. A new terrorist threat emerging from Taliban-controlled post-withdrawal Afghanistan could severely damage Biden's foreign policy goals.

Cuba and Latin America: not so easy...

The idea of returning to the Obama era orientation toward Cuba, which aimed to establish a more amicable relationship with the island, was shelved when in early July the Cuban government violently suppressed protestors taking to the streets due to food and medicine shortages exacerbated by the pandemic. To the disappointment of some Cuban Americans who had hoped Biden might reverse the damage Trump had done to the process of normalizing Cuban-American ties, Biden has instead intensified sanctions against Cuban officials and pledged support for protestors. While the efforts are meant to protect and support the democratic rights of oppressed Cuban citizens, the strained relationship has had detrimental effects on some Cubans. Limited flights between the United States and Cuba, as well as tighter regulations on sending money to the island, have stifled Cuban Americans' abilities to aid their loved ones who are still in Cuba, and economic sanctions have been termed "economic asphyxiation" of the island by Cuban president Miguel Díaz-Canel.[89] In light of these difficulties, attempted migration to the United States by fleeing Cubans has majorly increased, rising from 12,502 individuals and 1,440 families in the 2019 fiscal year to 21,453 individuals and 4,718 families in the 2020 fiscal year.[90]

However, though some argue that normalizing relations is the best policy response, others (including, most notably, Chairman of the Senate Foreign Relations Committee Robert Menendez, the son of Cuban immigrants himself) believe

---

[88] Rahna Epting and Stephen Miles, "Don't Listen to the Pundits: Withdrawing from Afghanistan Is Incredibly Popular," *Newsweek*, June 16, 2021 https://www.newsweek.com/dont-listen-pundits-withdrawing-afghanistan-incredibly-popular-opinion-1600877 [accessed August 12, 2021].

[89] Jen Kirby, "Biden's Cuba Policy Is Suddenly in the Spotlight," *Vox*, July 14, 2021, https://www.vox.com/22573703/biden-cuba-protests-trump [Accessed August 10, 2021].

[90] Ernesto Londoño and Frances Robles, "Biden Ramps Up Pressure on Cuba, Abandoning Obama's Approach," *The New York Times*, August 9, 2021, https://www.nytimes.com/2021/08/09/world/americas/cuba-government-biden-pressure.html [Accessed August 10, 2021].

the administration should push the Cuban government more aggressively to demand democratic reforms with more sanctions or, according to some, military action.[91] It is likely Biden's approach will continue to lie somewhere between those two options. The policy challenge now for the Biden administration is to find ways to punish the Cuban government without inflicting collateral harm upon the people. The policy challenge for the Biden administration will be to support the Cuban people without also propping up the government. But crafting policies that help the people while pressuring the regime will continue to be an immense challenge.

Addressing the crisis in Cuba is important as a humanitarian obligation but also to stem the increased migration flows coming from the island. Biden's policy toward Cuba and much of the rest of Latin America, especially the Central American countries of Guatemala, Honduras, and El Salvador, rests on this goal of alleviating root problems in the sending countries so fewer people are compelled to flee to the United States. These initiatives include both short term relief for extreme weather events and longer-term projects that focus on problems like poverty and crime.

As noted in Chapter 3, Biden assigned Vice President Kamala Harris to take the lead on Central American issues, and she traveled there in June 2021 to meet with government officials and to bring the message that people should think twice before heading north to the U.S. border. As Harris embarked on this project, she faced several obstacles. The first is the potential unwillingness of the governments of the Central American countries to collaborate with the United States. For example, on July 27, the Biden administration suspended cooperation with Guatemala's Attorney General's Office after the agency fired its top anti-corruption prosecutor. The Biden administration explained it had "lost confidence" in the country's willingness to fight corruption.[92] Without the Guatemalan government's cooperation, corruption and the economic strife and violence it brings will continue to be a major issue in the country despite the efforts of the United States.

Secondly, the financial aid allotted to the Central American countries may not reach the intended beneficiaries or may not be provided in forms that are helpful to the impoverished. For example, despite Guatemala receiving over

---

[91] Carmen Sesin, "Cuba Policy Is Domestic Policy. It's a Tough Spot for Biden." *NBC News*, August 6, 2021, https://www.nbcnews.com/news/latino/biden-takes-steps-cuba-policy-cuban-americans-say-want-see-forceful-ac-rcna1595 [Accessed August 10, 2021].

[92] Elliot Spagat, "Harris Releases Strategy to Tackle Migration's Root Causes," *AP News*, July 29, 2021, https://apnews.com/article/joe-biden-immigration-62c0488da2f232b812fdb7174ec0df6f [Accessed August 10, 2021].

$1.6 billion in American aid through the 2010s, poverty rates, malnutrition, and corruption have all risen.[93] Funding to Honduras is also risky, as the country's president has been linked to drug trafficking and accused of embezzling aid money in the past.[94] And, like in Cuba, the El Salvadoran government has been accused of suppressing democracy and human rights.[95] Biden and Harris are in a tough spot, measured against their promise to develop policies that will benefit the citizens of the relevant Latin American countries without also supporting their governments and corruption. The result could be little progress on improving the lives of citizens in the Central American nations and consequently failing to reduce pressures on the border.

Immigration: policy may not produce substantial results for a long time

Despite the executive orders passed in his first 100 days, immigration policy continues to be a hot-button topic in the United States and will likely remain a large influence on the moral compass of Biden's presidency, particularly in the wake of the forced Afghan exodus. Typically, the flow of migrants slows during the summer months because of the heat, but the reactivation of the asylum system, the reopening of borders, and the persistent root causes in Central America caused a massive spike in numbers in the summer of 2021. According to Customs and Border Protection, there was a record number 188,829 migrant encounters at the border in the month of June 2021. Along with a surge in unaccompanied children and whistleblowing complaints.[96] Even with Biden promising that humanitarian endeavors would ground his immigration policy, asylum seekers have few options, making the entire process, as an immigration attorney calls it, a "communications disaster."[97] It will be the ultimate test for Biden's administration to

---

[93] Natalie Kiteroeff and Michael Shear, "U.S. Aid to Central America Hasn't Slowed Migration. Can Kamala Harris?" *The New York Times*, June 6, 2021, https://www.nytimes.com/2021/06/06/world/americas/central-america-migration-kamala-harris.html [Accessed August 10, 2021].
[94] Ibid.
[95] Ibid.
[96] Michael D. Shear and Eileen Sullivan, "Biden Faces New Pressure on Immigration," *The New York Times*, August 2, 2021. https://www.nytimes.com/2021/07/16/us/politics/migrant-families-homeland-security.html [accessed August 10, 2021].
[97] Priscilla Alvarez, "Biden's immigration plan runs into on-the-ground realities," *CNN Politics*, August 6, 2021. https://www.cnn.com/2021/08/06/politics/us-mexico-border-biden/index.html [accessed August 10, 2021].

navigate and reform the immigration system while facing heavy criticism from all sides of the political spectrum.

While the long-term goal is to solve the root of the problem in Central America, particularly in Guatemala, El Salvador, Honduras, and Nicaragua, the major short-term goal of the Biden administration is to reverse inhumane Trump-era immigration practices. Title 42, a public health law implemented under Trump during the pandemic to expel migrants at the border, remains the most urgent yet controversial order to rescind. Since March 2020, over 973,000 of 1.3 million migrants were denied asylum through this public health mandate.[98] Biden's task is complicated by the fact that his decision will receive strong backlash and encounter new challenges no matter what course he takes.

If he keeps Title 42 in place, he would lose the support of his own political party, including progressive Democrats, who argue that the health law has failed to serve as a deterrent to migrants and remind Biden that he will never be immune to Republican attacks.[99] And he could also lose critical support from migrant advocacy groups, who provide legal services to migrants and unaccompanied children – a loss that would invite even more criticism toward his administration.[100] Not only do these progressive and activist groups call for a revocation of the law, but they also disapprove of the alternatives Biden has put forth like "expedited removal" and ankle monitors.[101]

When Biden faces these left-wing critics, he also alienates key allies and frustrates global leaders, including Filippo Grandi, United Nations High Commissioner for Refugees.[102] Additionally, while keeping the law in place is part of the Republican agenda, it also gives Republicans another statistic to hold against Biden: Title 42, expelling migrants to Mexico and thus giving them the chance for multiple crossings, inflates the number of arrests at the border.[103]

Alternatively, if Biden removes Title 42, he satisfies the Democratic left, but he must then deal with the challenges that arise with hundreds of thousands of migrants seeking asylum. He could let the migrants into the United States until the situation is resolved through a court hearing, but these processes can take years to resolve, and expelling a migrant after a long period of time could

---

98 Biden Faces New Pressure... op cit.
99 Ted Hesson, "Biden kept a Trump-era border policy in place – that was a mistake, allies say," *Reuters*, July 7, 2021. https://www.reuters.com/world/us/biden-kept-trump-era-border-policy-place-that-was-mistake-allies-say-2021-07-07/ [accessed August 10, 2021].
100 Ibid.
101 Ibid.
102 Biden Faces New Pressure... op cit.
103 Analysis: Biden kept a Trump-era border... op cit.

label Biden's immigration policy as "catch and release" 2.0.[104] Alternatively, Biden could increase the number of detention centers to temporarily hold illegal migrants, but not without consequence The world saw a glimpse of this route when he partially lifted Title 42 for unaccompanied children: it demonstrated that the U.S. government does not yet have adequate resources to house and care for high numbers of migrants.[105] While Biden faces criticism from Democrats and activists by upholding the health law, his alternate route would also spark charges that the president is reverting to Trump-era inhumane policies. In sum, Title 42's resolution will be a major factor in determining Biden's final grade on immigration policy, and the chances of an uncontroversial outcome look slim considering he faces hostile responses with every course of action.

Although his enlightened immigration outlook renewed Democratic hopes, Biden is quickly running into the hurdles that have stumped American presidents for years. No path is clear cut. A *Foreign Policy* columnist has argued that the biggest challenge "will be reversing the thousand-odd regulatory rulings passed under Trump's tenure with the goal of making immigration as difficult as possible."[106] The complexity of the system was painfully demonstrated by the Taliban takeover in Afghanistan and the thousands of Afghan citizens who had worked for the United States in various capacities unable to exit the country. The Afghan case is not a "normal" part of the immigration policy challenge, but it adds to the obstacles facing the Biden administration in this area.

The Biden administration may need to throw all its resources into formulating an effective and humanitarian alternative to Title 42, ideally capturing the much-needed support of Democrats and migrant activists while also weaving around legal barriers set up by Republicans. With a new system in place, Biden could then look to tackle the root of the problem in Central America.

Politically, the influx of refugees and asylum seekers from Afghanistan has created new problems. Republican critics of the president within days of the Taliban seizure of power charged that bringing large numbers of Afghan citizens to the United States was intended to produce more votes for the Democratic Party. This guarantees that immigration issues will continue to be complicated by politicization of the issue.

---

[104] Biden Faces New Pressure... op cit.
[105] Ibid.
[106] James Traub, "Biden's Immigration Plan Exists on Paper, Not in Reality," *Foreign Policy*, April 26, 2021. https://foreignpolicy.com/2021/04/26/bidens-immigration-plan-exists-on-paper-not-in-reality/ [accessed August 10, 2021].

Counterterrorism: terrorist threats with roots abroad and at home

President Biden has assured that U.S. intelligence will maintain its capability to detect and eliminate future terrorist threats arising in a Taliban-controlled Afghanistan. A U.S. intelligence report released on April 13, 2021 assessed that neither al-Qaeda nor other terrorist groups pose an *immediate* threat to the United States.[107] Nonetheless, the Taliban, which began rapidly gaining territory in Afghanistan in summer of 2021, remains closely aligned with al-Qaeda and already harbors terrorist elements in the country, according to a June 2021 report released by the United Nations.[108] Criticizing the Doha Agreement for Bringing Peace to Afghanistan, a deal signed between the United States and the Taliban on February 29, 2020, Afghanistan's now-former president, Ashraf Ghani, said, the "Taliban have no intention and willingness for peace."[109] Now that U.S. forces are no longer on site to assist in intelligence collection and counterterrorism efforts, al-Qaeda and other terrorist groups could be given free reign by the Taliban to rebuild their leadership networks and capabilities. The chaos in Afghanistan could create new obstacles in the way of reestablishing American international leadership, as the process of ending "forever wars" could appear to be risking "forever terrorism."

On the domestic side, Biden has become the first president in the nation's history to announce a strategy to target domestic terrorist threats.[110] The plan, however, has already garnered criticism from human rights activists with concerns that the policy could harm the most vulnerable populations, people of color and other minorities, who are the ones that need the protection against violent white extremism. An unclassified expert assessment of domestic terrorism in the United States, released in March 2021, found that "the two most lethal elements of today's domestic terrorism threat are (1) racially or ethnically motivat-

---

107 Julian Barnes and Eric Schmitt, "Will Afghanistan Become a Terrorist Haven Once Again?" *The New York Times*, April 13, 2021, https://www.nytimes.com/2021/04/13/us/politics/afghanistan-terrorism-threat.html [accessed August 11, 2021].
108 Lisa Curtis, "Taliban Ascendance in Afghanistan Risks Return of Global Terrorist Hub," *Just Security*, July 23, 2021, https://www.justsecurity.org/77550/taliban-ascendance-in-afghanistan-risks-return-of-global-terrorist-hub/ [accessed August 11, 2021].
109 Ibid.
110 Harsha Panduranga, "Why Biden's Strategy for Preventing Domestic Terrorism Could Do More Harm Than Good," *Brennan Center for Justice*, June 23, 2021, https://www.brennancenter.org/our-work/analysis-opinion/why-bidens-strategy-preventing-domestic-terrorism-could-do-more-harm-good [accessed August 11, 2021].

ed violent extremists who advocate for the superiority of the white race and (2) anti-government or anti-authority violent extremists, such as militia violent extremists."[111]

One component of the Biden administration's response has been to provide funds and support for local law enforcement to facilitate prevention efforts, including identifying people who may become violent and connecting them with mental health and social services. Civil rights activists believe that decades of research show that reliably identifying potentially violent individuals is not possible (qualifying factors include widespread traits such as mental health issues, having trouble at home or in relationships, and/or having a political or personal "grievance"). They are also concerned that this strategy will integrate more police involvement in mental health and social services and thereby increase bias and violence against minority groups.[112] Instead, groups like the Brennan Center advocate greater separation of the police from schools and other social institutions, as well as for adding specific safeguards against privacy and civil rights violations of minority groups directly into the plan.[113] For Biden to accomplish his goal of protecting against the growing threat of domestic terrorism without instead perpetuating harm against the groups that need the protection, he will need to reevaluate and rework his proposal to ensure it is effective and implemented without unintended consequences. This process of refining the approach suggests that no clear progress may be identifiable in the near term, preventing Biden from being able to claim success in this area.

Pandemic policy: anti-vaxxers/maskers risk Covid-19 resurgence

As discussed in Chapter 3, Biden pursued an aggressive and enhanced Covid plan consisting of high-volume vaccine rollout and economic stimulus. Most experts and White House officials predicted that the United States would be able to return to something resembling normalcy by the fall of 2021, but just when the country was on a downhill slide of cases, the ultrafast spreading Delta variant surfaced. With masks back and Covid cases climbing, the new strain posed a major setback to Biden's plans.

---

[111] "Fact Sheet: National Strategy for Countering Domestic Terrorism," *White House Briefing Room*, June 15, 2021, https://www.whitehouse.gov/briefing-room/statements-releases/2021/06/15/fact-sheet-national-strategy-for-countering-domestic-terrorism/ [accessed August 11, 2021].
[112] Panduranga, "Why Biden's Strategy."
[113] Ibid.

Getting most Americans vaccinated – the best way to stop Covid and its new Delta variant – remains the top priority of the administration, but rampant misinformation impedes that path. The partisan gap in vaccinations began under Trump, who repeatedly downplayed the severity of the virus, and continues to grow under right-wing media outlets like Fox News. Common myths including the belief that the quick development of the vaccine made it less safe or that it has long-term harmful health effects have all been debunked by reliable sources. Yet false information perpetuated by the administration's political opponents leads the United States in the complete wrong direction. U.S. Surgeon General Dr. Vivek Murthy called health misinformation "an urgent public health crisis" intensified by algorithms that pull Americans "deeper and deeper into a well of misinformation."[114] Running out of ways to overcome the cycle of misinformation, the Biden administration began advocating for a mandatory vaccination requirement, as well as imposing travel restrictions, mask mandates, and cash incentives. The problem, however, is that some Americans have made it clear that there is not anything the president can do to that will convince them to get vaccinated.

Another obstacle delaying the supposed return to normal revolves around the economy. Although the United States took a hard economic hit from the pandemic early on, the first half of 2021 saw stellar economic growth with increased consumer spending, widespread vaccine access, and the reopening of schools and businesses. However, the job market still lagged 6.8 million positions short of pre-pandemic levels.[115] With extended unemployment benefits ending on Labor Day in many states, it remained unclear how quickly people would return to jobs to which they had not previously returned, potentially due to the generous extra unemployment benefits. A continued economic recovery depends heavily on the strength of the job market, as the employment rate sways consumer spending. but the surge in the Delta variant along with uncertainty regarding future strains further complicated hopes for a sustained economic recovery.

While many Americans with widespread access to free vaccines have watched their bank accounts bounce back, much of the world remained entangled in the global health crisis. The United States and wealthy European countries snag-

---

114 "Press Briefing by Press Secretary Jen Psaki and Surgeon General Dr. Vivek H. Murthy," *White House Briefing Room,* July 15, 2021. https://www.whitehouse.gov/briefing-room/press-briefings/2021/07/15/press-briefing-by-press-secretary-jen-psaki-and-surgeon-general-dr-vivek-h-murthy-july-15-2021/ [accessed August 11, 2021].

115 Tim Tankersley and Jeanna Smialek, "Big Economic Challenges Await Biden and the Fed This Fall," *The New York Times,* August 3, 2021. https://www.nytimes.com/2021/08/03/business/economy/Biden-Federal-Reserve-economic-challenges.html [accessed August 11, 2021].

ged half of all vaccine doses, leaving poorer countries behind.[116] By mid-2021, only about 0.3% of all vaccines had been administered to the 29 poorest countries holding 9% of the global population.[117] Poorer countries desperately need vaccines, and the Biden administration has felt added pressure from the global economy to push pharmaceutical companies to supply more than a tiny fraction of vaccines across borders.[118] Building a more stable, global health network and improving transparency between nations would help limit the impact of future pandemics as well.

Despite the hopes of Dr. Fauci, the administration's leading pandemic expert, a return to normal continues to be pushed back with some new obstacles – the Delta variant – and some recurring obstacles – the reluctance of a substantial minority of Americans to get vaccinated. Some Americans apprehensive of the safety of the vaccine are waiting for FDA approval, which was announced only in August 2021. The timeline for the authorization of vaccines for children under 12 was still undetermined. And there is always the persistent fear that another strain of Covid could cultivate. In conclusion, the pandemic remains a major obstacle to the success of President Biden's attempt to present a sterling model to the world both in terms of the functioning of American democracy and policies that serve the international community as well.

Climate change: no time to waste

Addressing the dire crisis posed by climate change has been made a major priority of President Biden's administration, while also emphasizing that the measures he plans to implement will benefit average Americans economically. However, as the frequency and intensity of extreme weather events accelerates across the globe, from the Bootleg Fire raging in Oregon and polluting the air quality across the country to catastrophic flooding in Germany and wildfires in Greece and Turkey, a UN report outlining the urgent need to reverse climate change

---

116 Richard Pérez-Peña, "How Hard Could It Be to Vaccinate the Whole World? This Hard," *The New York Times,* May 3, 2021. https://www.nytimes.com/2021/05/03/world/global-coronavirus-vaccine-shortage.html [accessed August 11, 2021].
117 Peter S. Goodman, Apoorva Mandavilli, Rebecca Robbins, and Matina Stevis-Gridneff, "What Would It Take to Vaccinate the World Against Covid?" *The New York Times,* June 3, 2021. https://www.nytimes.com/2021/05/15/world/americas/covid-vaccine-patent-biden.html [accessed August 11, 2021].
118 How Hard Could It be to Vaccinate... op cit.

with drastic action has ramped up the pressure on Biden to gain congressional passage of substantial environmental legislation. The report combined over 14,000 studies to show that the United States and the rest of the world are running out of time, as the critical global heating threshold of 1.5C is set to be surpassed much earlier than previously predicted – within a decade, according to the report.[119]

The Senate passage of a bipartisan $1 trillion infrastructure bill took steps toward environmental reform, with stipulations to build a national network of electric vehicle chargers, electrify thousands of schools and transit buses to reduce emissions, manufacture zero emission vehicles, upgrade power infrastructure with thousands of miles of transmission lines to facilitate the expansion of renewable energy (the single largest investment in clean energy transmission in American history), and allot $21.5 billion to create an Office of Clean Energy Demonstrations as well as funds for resiliency projects.[120] Still, climate groups are highly critical of the legislation, which also grants a new liquid natural gas plant in Alaska billions in loan guarantees and produces waivers that weaken environmental reviews of construction projects. Further, about half of the funding allocated for clean-running buses and cars can be used for vehicles powered by cleaner-burning fossil fuels, which is preferable to diesel but still not as clean as electric buses or vehicles with no carbon emissions.[121] Not delivering legislation commensurate with the threat and urgency posed by climate change poses obstacles to the domestic success of his approach and potentially therefore of derivative international leadership on environmental issues.

Democrats also have a $3.5 trillion budget plan prepared that would significantly slash emissions among its other measures, an important step for the country that is the world's second-largest carbon emitter after China. But Biden and the Democrats in Congress will need to push the bill through before the midterm elections in 2022, when the party could lose its slim majority in either or both the Senate and the House. As Republicans have consistently aligned

---

119 Oliver Milman, "UN Climate Report Raises Pressure on Biden to Seize a Rare Moment," *The Guardian*, August 10, 2021. https://www.theguardian.com/us-news/2021/aug/10/un-climate-report-joe-biden-us-response [accessed August 12, 2021].
120 "Fact Sheet: President Biden Announces Support for the Bipartisan Infrastructure Framework," *The White House Briefing Room*, June 24, 2021, https://www.whitehouse.gov/briefing-room/statements-releases/2021/06/24/fact-sheet-president-biden-announces-support-for-the-bipartisan-infrastructure-framework/ [Accessed August 10, 2021].
121 Leslie Kaufman, "Climate Groups Claim Infrastructure Bill's Green Energy Spend Is a Gift to Oil Companies," *World Oil*, August 9, 2021, https://www.worldoil.com/news/2021/8/9/climate-groups-claim-infrastructure-bill-s-green-energy-spend-is-a-gift-to-oil-companies/ [accessed August 10, 2021].

with the fossil fuel industry in opposition to environmental regulations, loss of a Democratic majority in Congress would virtually end any possibility of meaningful progress on climate change. Much of the difficulty in ensuring the bill will pass before the midterm elections rests on moderate Democratic senators like Joe Manchin and Kyrsten Sinema, both of whom who criticized the scope and expense of the proposed bill.

Beyond domestic obstacles, Biden is faced with the task of guiding international cooperation on this crisis of global scale. When the United Nations Climate Change Conference convenes in Glasgow on November 1, 2021, the United States will struggle to reclaim leadership on climate change following four years of Trump's climate denial and non-cooperation. The European Commission announced plans on July 14, 2021, to put the bloc's 27 member states on track for carbon neutrality by 2050, with proposals to tax jet fuel, ban gasoline and diesel-powered vehicles within two decades, and raise funds to help lower-income households accelerate this transition from fossil fuels to clean energy.[122] Most notably, the package also creates a system of tariffs on some goods imported from non-EU countries, including the United States, with weaker climate laws in order to incentivize other nations to adopt similar policies.[123] Biden has already pushed back against this potential carbon tax, hoping to avoid another trade war. Critics of the policy claim that the taxes will harm consumers and result in poorer populations paying larger shares of the costs of decarbonization – especially if non-EU countries retaliate with their own tariffs and thus afflict European exporters. Thus, in the international arena as well, Biden must walk a fine line of pushing aggressive-enough climate legislation to affect significant change without generating public discontent and pushback over the costs of doing so.

Domestic "soft power" issues: economic revival depends on pandemic control

Biden's goal of "building America back better" depends to a great extent on whether the economy will cooperate. As noted above, by mid-2021, the stimulus packages intended to spark a recovery from the depressing influence of the pandemic had made positive contributions. A major obstacle to the continuation of

---

[122] Ishaan Tharoor, "Europe's Climate Plans Could Provoke Friction with U.S." *The Washington Post*, July 16, 2021, https://www.washingtonpost.com/world/2021/07/16/biden-eu-climate-friction/ [accessed August 10, 2021].
[123] Ibid.

the rebuilding process was Republican opposition to the next step: Biden's infrastructure package. To get a bipartisan approach, Biden agreed to split the package into traditional "hard" infrastructure (roads, bridges, electric grid, and other utilities) and human "soft" infrastructure (climate change, education, health care, and other social safety net items). He won a big victory in August 2021 when a bipartisan majority in the Senate passed a substantial hard infrastructure measure. The soft infrastructure measure clearly was not going to win any Republican support, and therefore could move forward only with solid support from all Democrats in the House and Senate, some of whose support would depend on reducing the cost of the programs.

A new factor entering the debate was steadily increasing inflation in the American economy. The stimulus had worked but its impact on economic growth, combined with other factors including material and labor shortages, was adding to growing inflation as a possible obstacle to Biden's building back program. While Republicans had demonstrated no concern about the impact on the deficit of Trump spending and tax policies, they returned to a traditional Republican focus on inflationary government deficit spending to argue against Biden's programs. The fact that Biden's budget relied on funding new social programs by reversing some of the tax benefits wealthy Americans and corporations had received from a Republican majority during the Trump presidency provided additional motivation for GOP opposition.

Another potential obstacle was fully inside Biden's own party. The fact that he would have to negotiate serious compromises with the GOP to get programs like the infrastructure package passed meant weakening or abandoning objectives held dear by liberal Democrats. While party centrists were largely comfortable with the process, it created a continuing tension within the party, particularly among members of the House, where close to one half of the Democratic members belonged to the left-leaning progressive caucus.

Foreign policy based on strong, united nation: many threats to unity

Biden's America is unlikely to appear strong and united to the outside world so long as former president Trump continues to promote the big lie that he won the election, Republican members of congress quake in fear that Trump will "primary" them with pro-Trump candidates if they step out of line, and a significant minority of Americans continue to believe Trump's lies and provide him with financial and political support. Trump's deep imprint on the GOP presents a huge obstacle to Biden's aspirations, even though there have been some signs that his advocacy of bipartisan approaches to major national issues has won some support, despite Trump's opposition.

The Senate passage of a major infrastructure bill in August 2021 was a singular victory for Biden's bipartisan aspirations. To get some Republican senators to cross the aisle and support the measure, Biden had to accept that the measure focused mainly on "hard" infrastructure, such as roads, bridges, power systems, and other utilities. The Democratic desire, expressed most strongly by the party's liberal wing, for "soft" infrastructure funding for climate, education, health, and other human infrastructure spending be handled separately – because such spending would not attract any significant Republican support.

There obviously may be additional bipartisan successes down the road, but the deep divisions in American society and political system are likely to continue to throw up obstacles to Biden's hope to lead a more-or-less united America. Many of the continuing obstacles to that unity have deep structural and societal roots: racial and economic divisions being among the leading causes. Issues like the role of policing in America, how best to deal with rising crime, and the need for gun control all produce emotional splits among Americans and their political leaders.

One particularly imminent obstacle related to such divisions is the prospect of Biden's Democrats losing control of either or both the Senate and House in the 2022 mid-term elections. Losses of one or both could leave Biden's agenda dead in the water. Republican-dominated state legislatures around the country have, in 2021, been seeking to enhance the chance of such an outcome by passing new voting laws whose impact would largely reduce ballot box access to constituencies most likely to support Democratic candidates. This strategy, in and of itself, is divisive and a threat to liberal democracy. If the strategy is successful, Biden's desire to present the United States to the world as a model of representative democracy will be seriously undermined.

Restoring American leadership: still in question

Given Biden's record so far and the apparent obstacles to his goals, what are the chances that he will have achieved his objective of creating a new and respected leadership role for the United States, de-Trumping U.S. foreign policy? The obstacles discussed above present a challenging picture. Biden inherited a country that had abandoned international leadership almost completely. He promised to restore that leadership and, as we have shown, that goal cannot be met simply through nice words and effective diplomacy, even though those were good places to start. Now, as is said, the proof will be in the pudding.

Biden's administration will have to rebuild U.S. institutional structures, particularly the Department of State, that were so badly damaged by Trump. He has made a good start with strong political appointments in key positions, but his task was handicapped by his administration's failure to nominate candidates in a timely fashion and by the Senate delaying confirmation of important nominees – largely due to Republican obstructionism.

The president will also have to hope that American allies respond constructively to his revolutionary changes in U.S. foreign policy. Biden's agenda could be seriously undermined if domestic critics can argue convincingly that Biden's "soft" approach to issues like defense burdensharing has accrued no benefits for the United States. While foreign policy is unlikely to be a major issue in the 2022 midterm elections, Republicans could gain some traction with this issue if Biden cannot provide evidence to the contrary.

A new obstacle added to the list in the summer of 2021 was the Taliban takeover in Afghanistan and the disastrous consequences of the Taliban's surprisingly fast imposition of control. The question will be how successful the Biden administration will be in repairing the damage its handling of the crisis has done to U.S. credibility and moral standing abroad.

The next chapter examines the steps that President Biden might consider to restore American global leadership and the potential consequences of success or failure. It argues that de-Trumping U.S. foreign policy will depend very much on what happens inside the United States. This necessity is not only the case because Biden has pledged that his foreign policy would be built on the process of restoring and reinvigorating American democracy. It is the case because without reestablishing faith in the American liberal democratic model, Biden will have no chance of bringing back America's international leadership role.

Chapter 5
Why does it matter whether Biden brings America back?

De-Trumping U.S. foreign policy would require a fundamental return to a value-based approach to America's role in the world. Trump's attitude toward the U.S. role in the world was largely transactional: what do we (I) get for this? The two main competitors for global power and influence are both pursuing a transactional approach as well. Neither China nor Russia has a value base for their attempt to win place of pride internationally. They depend on coercive means, payment, and hard power – both nations act with the intent to maintain internal control and to gain international followings. They have little to offer the world in terms of a political system that provides individual liberty combined with the power to determine policy and leaders (liberal democracy) within a framework set in the rule of law and derivative institutions. The convergence of the Chinese, Russian, and Trumpian choice of transactional foreign policy approaches over liberal political values created a threat to which Biden is responding. According to summer 2021 reports, Russia was, even after Biden's warnings to Putin, continuing efforts to disrupt American democracy by distributing disinformation that supports Trumpian and radical right attempts to defeat Biden's goal of unifying the nation.[124]

In historical context

Biden's democracy agenda aligns perfectly with the values set out in the U.S. constitution and the subsequent history of the American republic. When they established the republic, the founding fathers sought to escape from the influence of the old world, particularly from British colonial rule. George Washington's 1796 farewell address told the story for more than a century. He warned

> [T]he great rule of conduct for us in regard to foreign nations is in extending our commercial relations, to have with them as little political connection as possible. So far as we have already formed engagements, let them be fulfilled with perfect good faith. Here let us stop. Europe has a set of primary interests which to us have none, or a very remote relation.

---

124 Julian E. Barnes, "Russian Disinformation Targets Vaccines and the Biden Administration," *The New York Times*, August 5, 2021. https://www.nytimes.com/2021/08/05/us/politics/covid-vaccines-russian-disinformation.html [accessed August 15, 2021].

Hence she must be engaged in frequent controversies, the causes of which are essentially foreign to our concerns …

… Why, by interweaving our destiny with that of any part of Europe, entangle our peace and prosperity in the toils of European ambition, rivalship, interest, humor or caprice?

It is our true policy to steer clear of permanent alliances with any portion of the foreign world; so far, I mean, as we are now at liberty to do it; for let me not be understood as capable of patronizing infidelity to existing engagements …

Taking care always to keep ourselves by suitable establishments on a respectable defensive posture, we may safely trust to temporary alliances for extraordinary emergencies.[125]

Following Washington's lead, Thomas Jefferson's 1801 inaugural address declared that the United States should seek "peace, commerce, and honest friendship with all nations, entangling alliances with none." Seen through the 1800 American political lens, the main challenge was to solidify America's democracy, seeking to build a more democratic political system in the new world to protect the country from the sorts of political systems against which the colonies had revolted.

World War I hinted at the possibility that the United States might not successfully defend its democracy though a form of splendid isolation. Having fought successfully in that war, the United States chose to return to a more internally focused agenda. But the rise of Hitler and WWII made it clear that illiberal developments in Europe and around the globe could, in fact, threaten the American republic. It also led many Americans to accept that a more active and engaged United States in world politics would be required if its experiment in democracy was to survive.

Despite a strong residue of isolationist sentiment, post-WWII America chose international involvement through the United Nations and subsequently the North Atlantic Treaty Organization. The United States took the lead in creating the United Nations, a global collective security organization, which the country had previously passed on in rejecting membership in the League of Nations after the First World War. In helping found NATO, it accepted the role as the leading member of a collective defense organization with a mandate for defending key American values: individual liberty, democracy, and the rule of law, all specified in the North Atlantic Treaty.

---

125 George Washington, *Washington's farewell address. Delivered September 17th, 1796*, New York: D. Appleton and company, 1861. Available at: https://archive.org/details/washingtonsfa00wash/page/20/mode/2up [accessed August 31, 2021].

It could be, and has been, argued[126] that post-World War II America got carried away with its democracy agenda, becoming too full of itself and its contributions to world peace to see its own failings. There certainly is some demonstrable truth to this statement, and America's failed interventions in Vietnam and now Afghanistan provide the prime examples.

Author Andrew Bacevich, a retired U.S. Army officer whose son was killed serving in Iraq, has argued that both Republican and Democratic administrations for far too long have proudly promoted a view of the United States as an "exceptional" nation, standing above other countries in its virtue and accomplishments. He sees this American self-perception as having created the rationale and political support for an imperial policy that leads to "forever wars." According to Bacevich, "...regardless of whether our self-inflicted contemporary apocalypse leads to renewal or further decline, the United states will find itself obliged to revise the premises informing America's role in the world. Put simply, basic U.S. policy must change."[127] The new model that he recommends is one of virtually complete withdrawal of American power resources from the world and concentration on repairing and reforming the American democracy. On the latter point, he is in some ways close to the goals articulated by the Biden administration, even though he rejects Biden's view that the United States should engage in the world as a defender and promotor of democracy. To Bacevich, this global role is exactly what has gotten the United States in over its head.

Despite the telling nature of Bacevich's critique of the United States – refined over the years with a trail of books and articles – he may simply go too far beyond what is pragmatic and even sensible in the near term. Bacevich recommends, for example, that the United States begin a phased withdrawal from NATO. Withdrawal, of course, would mean stepping away from the values represented by the alliance, but Bacevich sees NATO as simply a military alliance and does not believe that either the United States or the alliance are particularly representative of those values. Some, including this author, find this suggestion seriously lacking. At a time when liberal democracy is under threat both externally and internally, it seems a poor time to weaken the alliance among nations that still aspire to the values represented by the Western system, even if they do not all fulfill the promise all the time. Rather than stepping away from NATO, it might make more sense to constrain American deployment of hard power to a more limited universe while expanding its soft power, in part by repairing its

---

126 A very comprehensive example is A. G. Hopkins, *American Empire: A Global History*, Princeton: Princeton University Press, 2018.
127 Andrew Bacevich, *American Apocalypse, America's Role in the World Transformed*, New York: Henry Holt & Company, Inc., 2021.

own democracy, as argued here, and strengthening all ties with democratic allies.

By way of contrast, there is good cause to look at successful products of the American instinct to try to spread its liberal democratic ideology and capitalist model. Surely, the success of that model in Japan and Germany after WWII was produced mostly by the Japanese and West Germans themselves. But they received strong encouragement from a victorious American power that chose to promote reconstruction of its former adversaries rather than take punitive action against them, as other nations had done to Germany after WWI. In historical terms, American generosity in these cases was not the norm for international relations and should be cause for a degree of both American pride and foreign appreciation.

The bottom line

The bottom line for evaluating President Biden's chance of success in de-Trumping U.S. foreign policy and bringing America back is complex. It involves a nexus of foreign and domestic factors, several of which are beyond Biden's control. But success would likely involve some combination of the following policy approaches:

— Collaborating with allies in Europe and Asia to develop common approaches to security challenges and shared responsibilities and burdens in dealing with those challenges; encouraging allies to respond with increased efforts to Biden's concept of working with other nations, particularly U.S. allies, to deal with international security and other challenges, including dealing with fallout from the lost war in Afghanistan.
— Sustaining Biden's democracy initiative domestically to restore the American model in practice at home while supporting allied democracies abroad; being very judicious about promoting liberal democracy in nations ill-equipped to deal with the challenges that establishing and preserving such systems present.
— Working with international institutions to encourage their decisions and actions to take U.S. national interests and perspectives into account.
— Producing policies toward China and Russia that gain allied support and are politically sustainable domestically: this will require sophisticated application of military capabilities, financial and economic tools, and creative diplomacy built around policies that combine defense and deterrence with cooperation when such cooperation is possible and in the U.S. interest.

- Negotiating toward a new arrangement with Iran that will deter or at least delay Tehran's acquisition of nuclear weapons and dissuade Iran from supporting terrorist activities in the region.
- Managing the relationship with Saudi Arabia by considering the country's strategic importance to the United States while encouraging its movement toward a more liberal humanitarian form of governance.
- Sustaining U.S. support for Israel while promoting a more progressive Israeli approach toward the Palestinians.
- Pursuing relations with Taliban-led Afghanistan with a combination of carrots and sticks designed to diminish prospects for the regime once again hosting terrorist groups that could threaten the United States or its allies; at the same time, responding as possible to the inevitable humanitarian crisis in the country, particularly in concert with other nations and international organizations, in a manner that does not get the United States enmeshed in internal Afghan affairs.
- Promoting progress in Cuba toward a more open political system with which the United States could entertain broader intergovernmental and interpersonal relations.
- Helping Latin American countries reduce the incentives for their populations to seek entry to the United States by addressing poverty, corruption, crime, and other internal push factors there.
- Demonstrating effective management of the southern border to reduce risks of threatening or illegal activities while establishing humane conditions for the reception and processing of legitimate refugees and asylum seekers.
- Investing in facilities and programs to facilitate the resettlement and integration of large numbers of Afghan citizens forced out of their country by Taliban threats to those who worked with or for the United States and its allies.
- Working with allies to counter international terrorist threats, seeking where possible to get at the roots of terror and help nations mitigate those causes; in the United States, responding to the growing threats posed by white nationalists and anti-government groups with effective intelligence, smart policing, and judicial action.
- Continuing to fight the Covid-19 virus and its variants with vaccine deployment and masking policies, as well as countering misinformation campaigns; in parallel with an active domestic anti-pandemic policy, cooperating with allied nations and international institutions to support less developed nations in containing Covid spread, which is ultimately required to mitigate future spread at home.
- Aggressively pursuing domestic programs and international cooperation to counter climate change with programs and incentives to reduce carbon emis-

sions and increase reliance on low greenhouse gas energy sources; making the United States an international leader both diplomatically and in practice.
— Placing a strong emphasis on sustaining an economy that benefits all Americans, opening opportunities in both education and employment; ensuring equitable treatment by the legal and legislative systems of all Americans, regardless of race or other discriminatory factors; working to eliminate all forms of discrimination based on sexual orientation or identity.

If the Biden administration is successful in most of these areas, it will have done well and will have re-established a degree of international respect. But there is one major hitch: if the Democrats are not able to maintain control of the House and Senate in the 2022 midterm elections, Biden's last two years of this term of office may find him simply managing the country rather than leading it. The elephant in the room remains his predecessor, and Trump's ability to control developments and the electoral success of the Republican Party. To continue to move toward his goal of bringing America back, Biden must demonstrate to the American people that his approach to governance is far more consistent with American democratic principles than the transactional approach of Donald Trump and that of either China or Russia.

Democracy at home, key to leadership abroad

It is important to ask whether the United States can guarantee the survival of its republic if it does not have a strong belief in the ideological foundation for its democracy. Biden's success internationally will depend on the outcome of his domestic objectives. As two American authors have concluded, "If Biden wants to bring about a democratic revival – to lead, as he constantly (and rightly) says, by the "power of our example" – he should focus on getting America's own house in order."[128]

Biden was correct to begin his democracy-building project at home. The suggestion that former president Trump at least inspired, if not masterminded, a coup attempt designed to keep himself in power makes it clear how important the homeland project is. America's own democracy will not be secure if a signif-

---

[128] Robert Manning and Mathew Burrows, "The problem with Biden's democracy agenda," *War on the Rocks*, July 27, 2021. https://warontherocks.com/2021/07/the-problem-with-bidens-democracy-agenda/ [accessed August 12, 2021].

icant minority of the American electorate remains willing to follow a political figure who conveys distortions and lies along with a chorus of fawning media and acolytes. Following a leader who relies on conspiracy theories and a fully indefensible set of lies poses serious threats to a political system that relies on open and accurately informed discussion and decisions. Thus, the mid-term elections in 2022 and presidential election in 2024 will be critical to the future of American democracy, not just to President Biden's agenda. The question will be whether truth will break through the wall of disinformation behind which some number of Americans stand in willful ignorance.

So, the ultimate success of Biden's democracy foreign policy objectives will rely most fundamentally on his ability to move his own country away from the authoritarian temptation and back toward American ideals. Until American allies can be certain that the United States has returned to a liberal democratic path, they will see American leadership as uncertain and unreliable, no matter what good words are produced by the Biden administration.

If Biden is not able to sustain the domestic political side of his agenda, the chances of accomplishing his goal of bringing America back internationally will be severely diminished. Already, while U.S. allies welcome the dramatic change from Trump to Biden as the head of the West's leading power, they harbor doubts. The disastrous end of the U.S. and allied presence in Afghanistan did not help. More importantly, however, America's friends and allies do not know if Biden will succeed and return to the presidency in 2025 (or support a like-minded Democrat to succeed him) or if Donald Trump or one of his political ilk will take the United States back to a more autocratic, transactional U.S. foreign and domestic policy. The fate of American democracy and therefore of U.S. leadership of the Western democracies will be on the line in the 2022 and 2024 elections. Biden cannot return the United States to its international leadership role unless he manages to move the United States away from its fascist temptations and back toward the tasks of reforming, refining, and strengthening its own liberal democracy. Biden will require the active support of like-minded liberal democrats around the world to achieve this goal.

Bibliography

Acemoglu, Daron, and James A. Robinson. *The Narrow Corridor: States, Societies, and the Fate of Liberty*. New York: Penguin Press, 2019.

Alvarez, Priscilla. "Biden's immigration plan runs into on-the-ground realities." CNN Politics. Last modified August 6, 2021. Accessed August 10, 2021. https://www.cnn.com/2021/08/06/politics/us-mexico-border-biden/index.html.

Appelbaum, Yoni. "'I Alone Can Fix It.'" The Atlantic. Last modified July 21, 2016. Accessed June 23, 2021. https://www.theatlantic.com/politics/archive/2016/07/trump-rnc-speech-alone-fix-it/492557/.

Bacevich, Andrew. *American Apocalypse, America's Role in the World Transformed*. Henry Holt & Company, Inc., 2021.

Bandow, Doug. "What Happens if North Korea Won't Deal with Joe Biden?" CATO Institute. Last modified June 25, 2021. Accessed August 7, 2021. https://www.cato.org/commentary/what-happens-north-korea-wont-deal-joe-biden.

Barnes, Julian E. "Russian Disinformation Targets Vaccines and the Biden Administration." The New York Times. Last modified August 5, 2021. Accessed August 15, 2021. https://www.nytimes.com/2021/08/05/us/politics/covid-vaccines-russian-disinformation.html.

Barnes, Julian E., and Eric Schmitt. "Will Afghanistan Become a Terrorism Safe Haven Once Again?" The New York Times. Last modified April 13, 2021. Accessed August 11, 2021. https://www.nytimes.com/2021/04/13/us/politics/afghanistan-terrorism-threat.html.

Beer, Tommy. "Ivanka's Trademark Requests Were Fast-Tracked In China After Trump Was Elected." Forbes. Last modified September 22, 2020. Accessed July 25, 2021. https://www.forbes.com/sites/tommybeer/2020/09/22/ivankas-trademark-requests-were-fast-tracked-in-china-after-trump-was-elected/?sh=19f1927f1d60.

Bennett, Brian. "Biden Administration Says Talks with Russia on Cyber Attacks Are Progressing. Privately, Staffers Are Skeptical." Time. Last modified July 8, 2021. Accessed August 9, 2021. https://time.com/6078997/biden-cyber-attacks-putin/.

Biden, Joe. "Remarks by President Biden at the 2021 Virtual Munich Security Conference." Speech presented at East Room, February 19, 2021. White House Briefing Room. Accessed July 13, 2021. https://www.whitehouse.gov/briefing-room/speeches-remarks/2021/02/19/remarks-by-president-biden-at-the-2021-virtual-munich-security-conference/.

Biden, Joe. "Remarks by President Biden on America's Place in the World." Speech presented at U.S. Department of State Headquarters, February 4, 2021. White House Briefing Room. Accessed July 12, 2021. https://www.whitehouse.gov/briefing-room/speeches-remarks/2021/02/04/remarks-by-president-biden-on-americas-place-in-the-world/.

Biden, Joe. "Remarks by President Biden on the Way Forward in Afghanistan." Speech presented at Treaty Room, April 14, 2021. White House Briefing Room. Accessed July 17, 2021. https://www.whitehouse.gov/briefing-room/speeches-remarks/2021/04/14/remarks-by-president-biden-on-the-way-forward-in-afghanistan/.

"The Biden plan to build back better by advancing racial equity across the American economy." Biden-Harris Campaign, Accessed July 18, 2021. https://joebiden.com/racial-economic-equity/.

Blinken, Antony J. "A Foreign Policy for the American People." Speech presented at Ben Franklin Room, March 3, 2021. U.S. Department of State. https://www.state.gov/a-foreign-policy-for-the-american-people/.

Brooks, Vincent, and Ho Young Leem. "A Grand Bargain With North Korea." Foreign Affairs. Last modified July 29, 2021. Accessed August 7, 2021. https://www.foreignaffairs.com/articles/united-states/2021-07-29/grand-bargain-north-korea.

Buckley, Chris, and Steven Lee Myers. "Biden's China Strategy Meets Resistance at the Negotiating Table." The New York Times. Last modified July 26, 2021. Accessed July 27, 2021. https://www.nytimes.com/2021/07/26/world/asia/china-us-wendy-sherman.html?action=click&module=In%20Other%20News&pgtype=Homepage.

Bump, Philip. "Robert Gates Thinks Joe Biden Hasn't Stopped Being Wrong for 40 Years." The Atlantic. Last modified January 7, 2014. Accessed June 27, 2021. https://www.theatlantic.com/politics/archive/2014/01/robert-gates-thinks-joe-biden-hasnt-stopped-being-wrong-40-years/356785/.

Congressional Research Service. *U.S.-China Strategic Competition in South and East China Seas: Background and Issues for Congress.* By Ronald O'Rourke. Report no. R42784. August 4, 2021. Accessed August 5, 2021. https://fas.org/sgp/crs/row/R42784.pdf.

Crowley, Michael, and Jennifer Schuessler. "Trump's 1776 Commission Critiques Liberalism in Report Derided by Historians." The New York Times. Last modified January 18, 2021. Accessed July 30, 2021. https://www.nytimes.com/2021/01/18/us/politics/trump-1776-commission-report.html%20[.

Curtis, Lisa. "Taliban Ascendance in Afghanistan Risks Return of Global Terrorist Hub." Just Security. Last modified July 23, 2021. Accessed August 11, 2021. https://www.justsecurity.org/77550/taliban-ascendance-in-afghanistan-risks-return-of-global-terrorist-hub/.

Czuczka, Tony. "U.S. Has More Ukraine Military Aid in Reserve, Biden Aide Says." Bloomberg. Last modified June 20, 2021. Accessed August 12, 2021. https://www.bloomberg.com/news/articles/2021-06-20/u-s-has-more-ukraine-military-aid-in-reserve-biden-aide-says.

Dalton, Toby. "The Most Urgent North Korean Nuclear Threat Isn't What You Think." Carnegie Endowment for International Peace. Last modified April 15, 2021. Accessed August 7, 2021. https://carnegieendowment.org/2021/04/15/most-urgent-north-korean-nuclear-threat-isn-t-what-you-think-pub-84335.

DeFede, Jim. "Joe Biden Confident He'll Turn Florida Blue, Says He'll Restore Obama-Era Cuba Policies In Exclusive CBS4 Interview." CBS Miami. Last modified April 27, 2020. Accessed July 17, 2021. https://miami.cbslocal.com/2020/04/27/cbs4-joe-biden-interview/.

Detrow, Scott, and Nathan Rott. "At Biden Climate Summit, World Leaders Pledge To Do More, Act Faster." National Public Radio. Last modified April 22, 2021. Accessed July 29, 2021. https://www.npr.org/2021/04/22/989491975/at-climate-summit-biden-stresses-u-s-commitment-and-economic-opportunity.

Einhorn, Robert. "The rollout of the Biden administration's North Korea policy review leaves unanswered questions." The Brookings Institution. Last modified May 4, 2021. Accessed July 14, 2021. https://www.brookings.edu/blog/order-from-chaos/2021/05/04/the-rollout-of-the-biden-administrations-north-korea-policy-review-leaves-unanswered-questions/.

Epting, Rahna, and Stephen Miles. "Don't Listen to the Pundits: Withdrawing from Afghanistan Is Incredibly Popular." Newsweek. Last modified June 16, 2021. Accessed August 12, 2021. https://www.newsweek.com/dont-listen-pundits-withdrawing-afghanistan-incredibly-popular-opinion-1600877.

Erlanger, Steven. "Biden Is Embracing Europe, but Then What? NATO and the E.U. Have Concerns." The New York Times. Last modified June 6, 2021. Accessed July 24, 2021. https://www.nytimes.com/2021/06/06/world/europe/biden-nato-eu-trump.html.

"Fact Sheet: National Strategy for Countering Domestic Terrorism." White House Briefing Room. Last modified June 15, 2021. Accessed August 11, 2021. https://www.whitehouse.gov/briefing-room/statements-releases/2021/06/15/fact-sheet-national-strategy-for-countering-domestic-terrorism/.

"Fact Sheet: President Biden Announces Support for the Bipartisan Infrastructure Framework." The White House Briefing Room. Last modified June 24, 2021. Accessed August 10, 2021. https://www.whitehouse.gov/briefing-room/statements-releases/2021/06/24/fact-sheet-president-biden-announces-support-for-the-bipartisan-infrastructure-framework/.

Farrow, Ronan. "Can Biden Reverse Trump's Damage to the State Department?" The New Yorker. Last modified June 17, 2021. Accessed August 12, 2021. https://www.newyorker.com/books/page-turner/can-biden-reverse-trumps-damage-to-the-state-department.

Fearnow, Benjamin. "Poll Shows US Image Problem in Europe Persists as Biden Embarks on Trip to Repair Ties." Newsweek. Last modified June 7, 2021. Accessed July 24, 2021. https://www.newsweek.com/poll-shows-us-image-problem-europe-persists-biden-embarks-trip-repair-ties-1598249.

Freedman, Lawrence. "Trump's Limited Legacy." H-Diplo/ISSF Policy Series 2021–42. Last modified June 25, 2021. Accessed June 25, 2021. https://issforum.org/roundtables/policy/ps2021-42.

Gannon, Kathy. "Top US general foresees Afghan civil war as security worsens." AP News. Last modified June 29, 2021. Accessed August 9, 2021. https://apnews.com/article/joe-biden-afghanistan-9636261069b03719d569b5cf9fe5e4e5.

Gaouette, Nicole, and Jennifer Hansler. "US and Germany reach deal on controversial pipeline that Biden sees as a Russian 'geopolitical project.'" CNN Politics. Last modified July 21, 2021. Accessed August 12, 2021. https://www.cnn.com/2021/07/21/politics/us-german-nord-stream-2-deal/index.html.

Garver, Rob. "With Massive Spending Plans, Biden Seeks to Remake Relationship Between Federal Government and Americans." Voice of America. Last modified April 29, 2021. Accessed July 29, 2021. https://www.voanews.com/usa/massive-spending-plans-biden-seeks-remake-relationship-between-federal-government-and-americans.

Gates, Robert M. *Duty: Memoirs of a Secretary at War.* New York: Alfred A. Knopf, 2014.

Gavel, Doug. "Joseph Nye on Smart Power." Harvard Kennedy School Insight. Last modified July 3, 2008. Accessed August 1, 2021. https://www.belfercenter.org/publication/joseph-nye-smart-power.

Gearan, Anne. "Biden, pulling combat forces from Iraq, seeks to end the post-9/11 era." The Washington Post. Last modified July 26, 2021. Accessed July 26, 2021. https://www.washingtonpost.com/politics/biden-iraq-911-era/2021/07/25/619c8fe6-ecb1-11eb-97a0-a09d10181e36_story.html?utm_campaign=wp_politics_am&utm_medium=email&utm_source=newsletter&wpisrc=nl_politics&carta-url=https%3A%2F%2Fs2.washingtonpost.com%2Fcar-ln-tr%2F343d379%2F60fe9ff79d2fda945a190b87%2F5af5daa19bbc0f225bccd808%2F9%2F51%2F60fe9ff79d2fda945a190b87.

German, Tracey. "Russia: Biden brings a new US challenge to Putin's backyard." The Conversation. Last modified November 10, 2020. Accessed August 9, 2021. https://theconversation.com/russia-biden-brings-a-new-us-challenge-to-putins-backyard-149765.

González, Marlon, and Zeke Miller. "From scarcity to abundance: US faces calls to share vaccines." AP News. Last modified April 24, 2021. https://apnews.com/article/health-business-government-and-politics-immigration-europe-f6875e3094b1a51e9e8fc8ee84529ef0.

Goodman, Peter S., Apoorva Mandavilli, Rebecca Robbins, and Matina Stevis-Gridneff. "What Would It Take to Vaccinate the World Against Covid?" The New York Times. Last modified June 3, 2021. Accessed August 11, 2021. https://www.nytimes.com/2021/05/15/world/americas/covid-vaccine-patent-biden.html.

Gramer, Robbie. "Can Biden Solve the North Korea Puzzle? Biden opened the door for talks with Kim Jong Un, but Pyongyang is playing hard to get." Foreign Policy. Last modified June 28, 2021. Accessed July 26, 2021. https://foreignpolicy.com/2021/06/28/biden-north-korea-kim-jong-un-nuclear-talks-diplomacy-fail-succeed/.

Hansler, Jennifer. "Top Democrat and European counterparts slam US-Germany deal on Nord Stream 2." CNN Politics. Last modified August 2, 2021. Accessed August 12, 2021. https://www.cnn.com/2021/08/02/politics/menendez-nord-stream-2-joint-statement/index.html.

Hesson, Ted. "Biden kept a Trump-era border policy in place – that was a mistake, allies say." Reuters. Last modified July 7, 2021. Accessed August 10, 2021. https://www.reuters.com/world/us/biden-kept-trump-era-border-policy-place-that-was-mistake-allies-say-2021-07-07/.

Hopkins, A. G., ed. *American Empire: A Global History.* Princeton, NJ: Princeton University Press, 2018.

Kaufman, Leslie. "Climate groups claim infrastructure bill's green energy spend is a gift to oil companies." World Oil. Last modified August 9, 2021. Accessed August 10, 2021. https://www.worldoil.com/news/2021/8/9/climate-groups-claim-infrastructure-bill-s-green-energy-spend-is-a-gift-to-oil-companies.

"Kim's sister says US interpreting signals from North Korea in 'wrong way.'" Nikkei Asia. Last modified June 23, 2021. Accessed August 7, 2021. https://asia.nikkei.com/Spotlight/N-Korea-at-crossroads/Kim-s-sister-says-US-interpreting-signals-from-North-Korea-in-wrong-way.

Kirby, Jen. "Biden's Cuba policy is suddenly in the spotlight." Vox. Last modified July 14, 2021. Accessed August 10, 2021. https://www.vox.com/22573703/biden-cuba-protests-trump.

Kitroeff, Natalie, and Michael D. Shear. "U.S. Aid to Central America Hasn't Slowed Migration. Can Kamala Harris?" The New York Times. Last modified June 6, 2021. Accessed August 10, 2021. https://www.nytimes.com/2021/06/06/world/americas/central-america-migration-kamala-harris.html.

Knickmeyer, Ellen, Matthew Lee, and Lolita C. Baldor. "US hosts high-level Saudi visit after Khashoggi killing." AP News. Last modified July 6, 2021. Accessed August 9, 2021. https://apnews.com/article/joe-biden-jamal-khashoggi-europe-middle-east-government-and-politics-fe49077941a4742da5dde3704d312927.

Lee, Matthew. "US Hits Iran for Delay in Nuclear and Prisoner Swap Talks." AP News. Last modified July 17, 2021. Accessed August 9, 2021. https://apnews.com/article/joe-biden-

middle-east-government-and-politics-iran-iran-nuclear-d910911862e274c701af2
fefcf20035e.
Mackinnon, Amy. "Russia Further Ramps Up Military Pressure on Ukraine." Foreign Policy. Last modified April 20, 2021. Accessed August 12, 2021. https://foreignpolicy.com/2021/04/20/russia-ukraine-black-sea-nato-biden-putin-zelensky-military/.
Maizland, Lindsay. "China's Repression of Uyghurs in Xinjiang." Council on Foreign Relations. Last modified March 1, 2021. Accessed August 6, 2021. https://www.cfr.org/backgrounder/chinas-repression-uyghurs-xinjiang.
Manning, Robert, and Mathew Burrows. "The Problem with Biden's Democracy Agenda." War on the Rocks. Last modified July 27, 2021. Accessed August 12, 2021. https://warontherocks.com/2021/07/the-problem-with-bidens-democracy-agenda/.
Massoud, Ahmad. "The mujahideen resistance to the Taliban begins now. But we need help." The Washington Post. Last modified August 18, 2021. Accessed August 18, 2021. https://www.washingtonpost.com/opinions/2021/08/18/mujahideen-resistance-taliban-ahmad-massoud/.
McBride, James. "President-Elect Biden on Foreign Policy." Council on Foreign Relations. Last modified November 7, 2020. Accessed July 12, 2021. https://www.cfr.org/election2020/candidate-tracker.
Milman, Oliver. "UN climate report raises pressure on Biden to seize a rare moment." The Guardian. Last modified August 10, 2021. Accessed August 12, 2021. https://www.theguardian.com/us-news/2021/aug/10/un-climate-report-joe-biden-us-response.
Murthy, Vivek H. "Press Briefing by Press Secretary Jen Psaki and Surgeon General Dr. Vivek H. Murthy," Speech, James S. Brady Press Briefing Room, July 15, 2021.
"NATO designates China a 'systemic' challenge." Nikkei Asia. Last modified June 15, 2021. Accessed August 5, 2021. https://asia.nikkei.com/Politics/International-relations/US-China-tensions/NATO-designates-China-a-systemic-challenge.
Naylor, Brian. "Biden White House Aims To Advance Racial Equity With Executive Actions." National Public Radio. Last modified January 26, 2021. Accessed July 30, 2021. https://www.npr.org/sections/president-biden-takes-office/2021/01/26/960725707/biden-aims-to-advance-racial-equity-with-executive-actions.
The New York Times. Last modified August 9, 2021. Accessed August 10, 2021. https://www.nytimes.com/2021/08/09/world/americas/cuba-government-biden-pressure.html.
Office of the Director of National Intelligence, Annual Threat Assessment of the US Intelligence Community, Rep. (Apr. 9, 2021) (Conf. Rep.). Accessed August 9, 2021. https://int.nyt.com/data/documenttools/annual-threat-assessment-report/5bd104278cd017bd/full.pdf.
O'Toole, Brian. "Rejoining the Iran nuclear deal: Not so easy." Atlantic Council. Last modified January 14, 2021. Accessed August 9, 2021. https://www.atlanticcouncil.org/in-depth-research-reports/issue-brief/rejoining-the-iran-nuclear-deal-not-so-easy/.
Pancevski, Bojan. "Why the Covid-19 Pandemic Weakened Far-Right Groups in Europe." The Wall Street Journal. Last modified June 30, 2021. Accessed August 12, 2021. https://www.wsj.com/articles/why-the-covid-19-pandemic-weakened-far-right-groups-in-europe-11625054400.
Panduranga, Harsha. "Why Biden's Strategy for Preventing Domestic Terrorism Could Do More Harm Than Good." Brennan Center for Justice. Last modified June 23, 2021. Accessed

August 11, 2021. https://www.brennancenter.org/our-work/analysis-opinion/why-bidens-strategy-preventing-domestic-terrorism-could-do-more-harm-good.

Parker, Ashley. "'Part of the club': Biden relishes revival of alliances that Trump dismissed." The Washington Post. Last modified June 15, 2021. Accessed July 24, 2021. https://www.washingtonpost.com/politics/biden-club-allies/2021/06/15/5a2fb206-cdad-11eb-9b7e-e06f6cfdece8_story.html.

Pérez-Peña, Richard. "How Hard Could It Be to Vaccinate the Whole World? This Hard." The New York Times. Last modified May 3, 2021. Accessed August 11, 2021. https://www.nytimes.com/2021/05/03/world/global-coronavirus-vaccine-shortage.html.

Rogin, John. "Biden must try harder to stop the coup in Tunisia." The Washington Post. Last modified July 26, 2021. Accessed July 27, 2021. https://www.washingtonpost.com/opinions/2021/07/26/biden-act-coup-tunisia-democracy/.

Ryan, Missy, Shane Harris, and Paul Sonne. "After troops leave Afghanistan, U.S. will face challenges maintain counterterrorism capability." The Washington Post. Last modified April 17, 2021. Accessed August 9, 2021. https://www.washingtonpost.com/national-security/afghanistan-withdrawl-qaeda-us-counterterrorism/2021/04/17/4a383b46-9eb1-11eb-8a83-3bc1fa69c2e8_story.html.

Saenz, Arlette, and Zachary Cohen. "Biden administration started outreach to North Korea last month, but country is unresponsive." CNN Politics. Last modified March 13, 2021. Accessed August 7, 2021. Google Search: Biden administration started outreach to North Korea last month, but country is unresponsive.

Sanger, David E., and Steven Erlanger. "For Biden, Europe Trip Achieved 2 Major Goals. And Then There Is Russia." The New York Times. Last modified July 15, 2021. Accessed July 25, 2021. https://www.nytimes.com/2021/06/17/world/europe/joe-biden-vladimir-putin-usa-russia.html.

Sesin, Carmen. "Cuba policy is domestic politics. It's a tough spot for Biden." NBC News. Last modified August 6, 2021. Accessed August 10, 2021. https://www.nbcnews.com/news/latino/biden-takes-steps-cuba-policy-cuban-americans-say-want-see-forceful-ac-rcna1595.

Shear, Michael D., and Zolan Kanno-Youngs. "In Another Reversal, Biden Raises Limit on Number of Refugees Allowed Into the U.S." The New York Times. Last modified May 3, 2021. Accessed July 28, 2021. https://www.nytimes.com/2021/05/03/us/politics/biden-refugee-limit.html.

Shear, Michael D., and Eileen Sullivan. "Biden Faces New Pressure on Immigration." The New York Times. Last modified August 2, 2021. Accessed August 10, 2021. https://www.nytimes.com/2021/07/16/us/politics/migrant-families-homeland-security.html.

Sloan, Stanley R. *Transatlantic Traumas: Has Illiberalism Brought the West to the Brink of Collapse?* Manchester University Press, 2018.

Snyder, Scott A. "Biden's Policy Review Leaves North Korea Challenge In Limbo." Council on Foreign Relations. Last modified May 19, 2021. Accessed July 17, 2021. https://www.cfr.org/blog/bidens-policy-review-leaves-north-korea-challenge-limbo.

Solis, Mireya. "U.S.-Japan relations in the era of Trump: Navigating the turbulence of 'America First.'" *Brookings Institution* 8, no. 24 (August 29, 2019). https://doi.org/10.32870/mycp.v8i24.669.

Spagat, Elliot. "Harris releases strategy to tackle migration's root causes." AP News. Last modified July 29, 2021. Accessed August 10, 2021. https://apnews.com/article/joe-biden-immigration-62c0488da2f232b812fdb7174ec0df6f.

Tankersley, Jim, and Jeanna Smialek. "Big Economic Challenges Await Biden and the Fed This Fall." The New York Times. Last modified August 3, 2021. Accessed August 11, 2021. https://www.nytimes.com/2021/08/03/business/economy/Biden-Federal-Reserve-economic-challenges.html.

Tepperman, Jonathan. "Biden's Dangerous Doctrine." Foreign Policy. Last modified July 21, 2021. Accessed August 5, 2021. https://foreignpolicy.com/2021/07/21/bidens-china-doctrine-decoupling-cold-war/.

Tharoor, Ishaan. "Europe's Climate Plans Could Provoke Friction with U.S." The Washington Post. Last modified July 16, 2021. Accessed August 10, 2021. https://www.washingtonpost.com/world/2021/07/16/biden-eu-climate-friction/.

Traub, James. "Biden's Immigration Plan Exists on Paper, Not in Reality." Foreign Policy. Last modified April 26, 2021. Accessed August 10, 2021. https://foreignpolicy.com/2021/04/26/bidens-immigration-plan-exists-on-paper-not-in-reality/.

"US and Russia hold arms control talks in Geneva." DW. Last modified July 27, 2021. Accessed August 9, 2021. https://www.dw.com/en/us-and-russia-hold-arms-control-talks-in-geneva/a-58671440.

"US-China relations: Details released of Biden's first call with Xi." BBC News. Last modified February 11, 2021. Accessed July 24, 2021. https://www.bbc.com/news/world-56021205.

Wike, Richard, Janell Fetterolf, and Mara Mordecai. "U.S. Image Plummets Internationally as Most Say Country Has Handled Coronavirus Badly." Pew Research Center. Last modified September 15, 2020. Accessed June 27, 2021. https://www.pewresearch.org/global/2020/09/15/us-image-plummets-internationally-as-most-say-country-has-handled-coronavirus-badly/.

Wootsen, Cleve R., Jr. "Harris wraps up a Latin America trip that featured sharp words to would-be immigrants." The Washington Post. Last modified June 8, 2021. Accessed July 28, 2021. https://www.washingtonpost.com/politics/kamala-harris-latin-america-trip/2021/06/08/279e360e-c859-11eb-81b1-34796c7393af_story.html.

Yee, Vivian. "Tunisia's President Holds Forth on Freedoms After Seizing Power." The New York Times. Last modified August 1, 2021. Accessed August 12, 2021. https://www.nytimes.com/2021/08/01/world/middleeast/tunisia-president-kais-saied.html?smid=tw-share.

Zakaria, Fareed. "The narrow path to liberal democracy." The Washington Post. Last modified July 29, 2021. Accessed August 2, 2021. https://www.washingtonpost.com/opinions/2021/07/29/world-is-reminding-us-that-democracy-is-hard/.

About the Author

Stanley R. Sloan is a Visiting Scholar in Political Science at Middlebury College, a Non-resident Senior Fellow in the Scowcroft Center of the Atlantic Council of the United States, and an Associate Fellow at the Austrian Institute for European and Security Policy. He has been a member of the Middlebury Winter Term Faculty for over 17 years and is the founding Director of the Atlantic Community Initiative. In 2016, he was invited to join the Dūcō experts consulting group. He has served as a Woodrow Wilson Foundation Visiting Fellow and a member of the Fulbright Specialists Program.

Before retiring from 32 years of government service, he was the Senior Specialist in International Security Policy at the Congressional Research Service (CRS) of the Library of Congress, where he previously served as head of the Office of Senior Specialists, division specialist in US alliance relations, and head of the Europe/Middle East/Africa section. Prior to joining CRS, he was a commissioned officer in the US Air Force and held several analytical and research management positions at the Central Intelligence Agency, including Deputy National Intelligence Officer for Western Europe. In 1973, he served as a member of the US Delegation to Negotiations on Mutual and Balanced Force Reductions in Vienna, Austria.

Stan has published hundreds of CRS Reports for Congress, as well as journal articles, book chapters and opinion editorials in major US and European publications on international security topics, US foreign policy, and European security. Stan lectures widely on international security topics in the United States and Europe and testified in September 2018 before the Senate Foreign Relations Committee on NATO and US interests.

His books and monographs include *Defense of the West: Transatlantic Security from Truman to Trump* (2020), *Transatlantic traumas: Has illiberalism brought the West to the brink of collapse?* (2018); *Defense of the West: NATO, the European Union and the Transatlantic Bargain* (2016); *Permanent Alliance? NATO and the Transatlantic Bargain from Truman to Obama* (2010); *NATO, the European Union, and the Atlantic Community: The Transatlantic Bargain Challenged* (2005); *The Use of U.S. Power: Implications for U.S. Interests* (2004) (coauthor); *NATO and Transatlantic Relations in the 21st Century: Crisis, Continuity or Change?* (2002); *The United States and European Defence* (2000); *The U.S. Role in the Twenty-first Century World: Toward a New Consensus* (1997); *NATO's Future: Beyond Collective Defense* (1995); *NATO in the 1990s* (1989); and *NATO's Future: Toward a New Transatlantic Bargain* (1985). He was rapporteur and study director for the North Atlantic Assembly's reports on "NATO in the 21st Century" (1998) and "NATO in the 1990s" (1988).

Sloan received his B.A. from the University of Maine and his Masters in International Affairs from the Columbia University School of International Affairs; he completed all but his dissertation for a Ph.D. at the School of International Service, American University; and is a distinguished graduate of the USAF Officers Training School. In 2005, he was named an Honorary Ancien of the NATO Defense College, where he has lectured for over three decades.

www.ingramcontent.com/pod-product-compliance
Lightning Source LLC
Chambersburg PA
CBHW051616230426
43668CB00013B/2127